for young women

MADE TO
CRAVE

Other books by the authors:

Lysa TerKeurst:

Made to Crave: Satisfying Your Deepest Desires with God,
Not Food

Made to Crave Devotional: 60 Days to Craving God,
Not Food

Becoming More Than a Good Bible Study Girl

Capture His Heart (for wives)

Capture Her Heart (for husbands)

Leading Women to the Heart of God

Living Life on Purpose

What Happens When Women Say Yes to God

What Happens When Women Walk in Faith

Who Holds the Key to Your Heart?

Shaunti Feldhahn:

For Young Women Only: What You Need to Know
about How Guys Think

For Young Men Only: A Guy's Guide to the Alien Gender

For Parents Only: Getting Inside the Head of Your Kid

For Women Only: What You Need to Know
about the Inner Lives of Men

For Men Only: A Straightforward Guide
to the Inner Lives of Women

For Women Only: In the Workplace

The Life-Ready Woman: Thriving in a Do-It-All World

The Veritas Conflict (fiction)

The Lights of Tenth Street (fiction)

for young women

MADE TO
CRAVE

SATISFYING YOUR DEEPEST
DESIRES WITH GOD

LYSA TERKEURST and
SHAUNTI FELDHAHN

ZONDERVAN®

ZONDERVAN.com/
AUTHORTRACKER
follow your favorite authors

ZONDERVAN

Made to Crave for Young Women
Copyright © 2012 by Lysa TerKeurst and Shaunti Feldhahn

This title is also available as a Zondervan ebook. Visit www.zondervan.com/ebooks.

Requests for information should be addressed to:
Zondervan, 5300 Patterson Ave. SE, Grand Rapids, Michigan 49530

ISBN 978-0-310-72998-3

Published in association with the literary agency of Fedd & Company, Inc., Post Office Box 341973, Austin, TX 78734.

Cover design: *Cindy Davis*
Cover photography: *Getty Images®*
Interior illustrations: *iStockphoto*
Interior design: *Ben Fetterley*

Printed in the United States of America

12 13 14 15 16 17 /DCI/ 19 18 17 16 15 14 13 12 11 10 9 8 7 6 5 4 3 2 1

Contents

A Note from Lysa

A special hello from my heart to yours. (Including a quick "hi" to any moms who may be peeking in!) I'm delighted to have a chance to go on a very personal journey with you ... a journey that has improved my life in many ways over the last few years, and I'm betting will change yours too.

You may be familiar with the book that came before this one, *Made to Crave: Satisfying Your Deepest Desires with God, Not Food.* It has spoken to a lot of women, but I heard from my teenage daughters and their friends that they wished there was a message that spoke directly to the deep longings, desires, and struggles that are unique to young women — struggles that go far beyond the food-related issues in the original book.

As a result, this journey of ours will examine three different ways Satan tries to lure you away from following God. I truly believe understanding the truths in this book will prepare you to make important decisions that will determine so much about the rest of your life.

The information tucked within these pages is tailored to meet you right where you are: as a girl who wants to walk the right path but finds that path is sometimes unclear, or who is interrupted by longings that pull you in other directions. Maybe you long for the acceptance of friends or the affection of a guy but sometimes feel lonely or rejected instead. Maybe you struggle with body image or a secret addiction to those yummy treats in the bakery aisle, and feel unhappy, guilty, or unhealthy. Perhaps you love, love, love that special feeling of buying a great new outfit at the store — and never end up feeling special permanently.

You are craving something *more*. And as you read through this book, you'll learn what that craving is and how to truly fill your heart so all those negative longings don't have a hold on you anymore. The good things will still be there; the bad ones simply won't be able to knock you off the path.

There is someone joining us in the pages of this book, and I'm so glad to welcome her here. I knew I had to enlist a coauthor who had written books for teenagers before, and my daughter Hope asked, "What about Shaunti Feldhahn?" Hope and I met Shaunti on a *very* fun cruise where we were both speaking, and what I loved about Shaunti is that she's not only a great Jesus girl, she's an accomplished social researcher who has spent many years interviewing men, women, and teenagers to find out how we all tick. You'll meet her in the pages ahead.

So are you ready to go on this journey with us? Our goal is to be careful but honest; understanding, but willing to ask you to accept nothing less than God's best for you.

Live Loved,
Lysa

PART ONE

Longing for More

chapter 1

She Saw No Need for God

Jenny had everything.

Gorgeous hair, flawless skin, and an infectious personality that won her the acceptance of friends and the interest of guys.

Her parents bought her nice clothes, gave her a cute little car, and didn't spare any expense when she threw parties at her house.

And of course, she had a chest that stuck out, a stomach that stayed flat, and long, lean legs.

I (Lysa) would be a fool to even think about liking the same boy as Jenny.

I had frizzy hair, unpredictable skin, and an infected personality where insecurities and a sense of not quite belonging ran deep.

I had to work to pay for my tank of a car and my off-brand clothes. I didn't do parties, at least not the kind where the cool people came. Often, it was just me, my friend Stephanie, and a few others, watching a video and pretending we didn't care that we weren't at the party down the street.

And of course I had a chest that stayed flat, a stomach that stuck out, and what I saw as stubby legs.

I seemed to fall short in every area while there was nothing Jenny ever seemed to want.

Hold on to that fact—it's important later.

Yes, I knew it wasn't smart to go after the same things Jenny wanted. I'd learned that lesson in a big way a few years before in the seventh grade.

With the same frizzy brown hair and knock-off clothes, I walked down the pea-green hallway of Raa Middle School. It was the day after student council elections, the day after my classmates confirmed what I'd so desperately feared: If you didn't have beauty, boobs, and a boyfriend, no one would vote for you. At least that's what it felt like at the time.

I shuffled toward my locker wishing I was invisible, keeping my eyes down while I made my feet continue walking. Finally, my locker was in sight. That glorious metal box was my one safe space in this world of catty girls with cute outfits and spiral-permed hair. The place where I could hide my face, let the tears slip, and pretend to be busy shuffling books.

But instead of finding respite in that tiny metal space, I found one of my election posters plastered to the front with the word *loser* scrawled across the front. How do you quickly hide a poster-sized proclamation by the world that you aren't good enough, cool enough, pretty enough, or accepted enough?

The sound of books dropping, girls laughing, tape ripping, and poster board crunching filled my ears as the sign resisted my attempts to ball it up small enough to fit into the mouth of the hallway trash can.

"Please fit, please fit, please fit! Oh, God, please help this stupid poster from this stupid election with my stupid face on it disappear into this stupid trash can!"

The bell rang. As all the "normal" people scampered past me, I heard Stephanie's voice like a dagger's death blow whisper, "Loser."

I turned and saw my one confidant, my one friend, my one secret holder being welcomed into Jenny's popular girl's circle. Stephanie's public rejection of me was her ticket in to the crowd we'd secretly loathed together. *Together.*

I sank down beside the stupid trash can where the stupid poster slowly untwisted on the ground in front of me. *Loser.*

I went home that afternoon and hid in my bedroom with an arsenal of junk food. Comfort was just a few mouthfuls away. But what comforted me in the moment compounded my feelings of helplessness as soon as the wrappers around me were empty.

Have you ever been there? I don't mean at the foot of a locker with a loser poster untwisting before you. I mean have you ever felt that everything would be better if only you had a life a little more like Jenny's? Have you ever wanted something so much you caught yourself thinking about it 24/7?

A better body? More acceptance from friends or attention from a boy? Money to buy things that get you noticed? Have you ever thought that if you just had *that,* you'd be happy?

What if I told you it's a lie? A lie hand-designed by Satan to pull you away from God and trap you in a life you really don't want. A great body, friends inviting you everywhere, boys hanging on your every word, and the ability to buy the cutest new outfits won't satisfy you. Sure, it may make you happy for a short while, but these feelings won't last.

In fact, after the initial rush of finding what you think you're looking for, you'll likely end up more hungry, more desperate, and more lonely than you ever expected.

I know because I have seen it time and time again. I watched how differently my life and Jenny's life played out. Time teaches valuable lessons.

For a while I chased what Jenny had, and in college I got some of it. I had the cool boyfriend, lots of friends, and — thanks to a running class — a more toned body.

But I still wasn't satisfied.

There was still this deep craving inside of me for something else. Something lasting. Something beyond what the shifting circumstances of the world had to offer.

Matthew 6:33 says, "But seek first his kingdom and his righteousness, and all these things will be given to you as well." The Greek word for *seek* in the original manuscript of the Bible is *zeteo*, and one of the meanings of that word is *to crave*.

In other words, everyone has a desire for "all these things" — love, acceptance, material things — but first and foremost we must always crave God. If we always have everything we long for in this world, we'll be numbed to the deeper and much more eternal longings of our heart. Only God can satisfy and fill those deep places in a lasting way.

Only God can give us what can never be taken away. His acceptance. His comfort. His provision.

Because Jenny always had what she wanted, because she

was not in a place of turning her longings toward God, she became numb to the deepest cries of her soul and followed her cravings in sad directions. She was always seeking, never truly finding.

Jenny dropped out of college when she got pregnant. She has experienced great heartbreak; she's endured the devastating end of not one but two marriages, and is currently living with her third boyfriend. She still parties on the weekends. Her once flawless skin now tells a tale of a hard life. She's in debt. She's restless. And she sees no need for God.

Do you remember earlier in this chapter where I told you to remember something? I said, "I seemed to fall short in every area while there was nothing Jenny ever seemed to want." At the time, I didn't realize just how much Jenny's great-looking surface hid a deep longing just like mine.

I suspect you know what it feels like to feel like you don't measure up. I bet you have felt the cravings for acceptance, comfort, and provision just like I did—just like Jenny secretly did.

If so, keep reading. What you're about to uncover in this book will change the way you look at your life, and protect you from searching your whole life for something that can only be found in God.

How, you ask?

That's exactly what we're about to uncover.

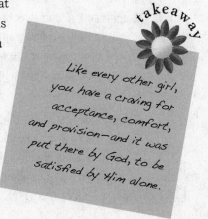

takeaway

Like every other girl, you have a craving for acceptance, comfort, and provision—and it was put there by God, to be satisfied by Him alone.

the action plan

At the end of each of the chapters ahead will be questions and ideas that might help you to apply or think further about what you have discovered in that chapter. If you'd like, you can use this book, and especially this section, as a personal devotional, reading pieces each day and reflecting on the appropriate questions.

For this chapter, find three things to accompany you on your journey:

Get a Bible. If you don't have a Bible, and it isn't possible to get one, find a good site online that you can use to look up Scripture passages. We like *BibleGateway.com* or *BlueLetterBible.com*, which allow you to see different translations of Scripture.

Get a friend. A journey is best walked with a friend, after all. And you will find great encouragement, inspiration, and comfort along the way if you use this book as a way of helping one another and having accountability with each other.

Get a journal. Many of the end-of-chapter sections will ask you to write down your thoughts, draw a picture, or make a list of things you are working on. Find a fun journal or just a simple notebook you can use.

What's Your *That*?

Shaunti and I want to ask you a question: What would it take to make you completely satisfied today? Would it be to have "that" boy ask you out? To be able to afford "that" wardrobe? To win "that" award or get accepted into "that" university? To be "that" size? To be "that" beautiful?

What is your "that"?

Often the script that plays in our head is, "If I had _____, I would be so happy."

Or what about its sister script? The one with the question marks at the end of each sentence and a really slick temptation as "the answer." You know the one I'm talking about:

Am I special? (I sure feel like it when that cute guy in class pays attention . . .)

Am I beautiful? (Maybe, if I could just fit into those jeans . . .)

Does anyone really like or notice me? (I guess so, when a lot of people comment on my Facebook post . . .)

Now, what if I assured you that there is a way to know for sure that you are special, beautiful, and noticed—because the One who created you and knows you better than anyone else has told you that you are? And what if I told you that the belief that anything else will make you truly satisfied is a lie? We looked at this lie in the last chapter. The problem is that it usually doesn't start out *feeling* like a lie; it might, in fact, give you that satisfied, happy feeling for a while. But the happy feeling will be temporary because the high of getting whatever it is you think you want will be temporary.

In fact ... this lie is hand-designed with your weakness in mind, to draw you away from God.

Not that any of those things I mentioned are wrong in and of themselves. But if the desire to have them pulls you away from God rather than draws you closer to Him, they become a temptation. A pull. A lure. A tactic handcrafted by Satan to get you to take a few steps away from God. And then a few more.

The focus of this book centers around ways Satan tries to distract us from God. He wants us to get legitimate needs met in an illegitimate way.

Satan comes after us in these three areas:

Emotional Desires

Physical Desires

Material Desires

It's the same three ways he came after Eve in the garden of Eden. Eve, the first woman, was tempted by Satan in the garden of Eden — a perfect place where Eve had everything she wanted. Well, almost everything. God told Eve and her husband, Adam, to not eat from the Tree of the Knowledge of Good and Evil. Though she had everything a girl could want, she set her eyes on what she was told she couldn't have. Satan lured Eve into the first sin, tempting her into taking the fruit from the forbidden tree and eating it.

I've learned a lot from this story about how Satan lures us.

It will taste good and feel good — physical desires

It will get you noticed — material desires

It will make you feel accepted and loved — emotional desires

Jesus was also tempted in these same three ways in a desert. But unlike Eve, Jesus didn't fall to Satan's temptation. While Eve focused on the forbidden object of desire, Jesus focused on the truth. Satan tries to tempt Jesus with physical desires, offering Him bread in the midst of a fast; Jesus resists by quoting a Bible verse. Satan offers Jesus material possessions, promising Him whole kingdoms; Jesus resists by quoting a Bible verse. Satan reminds Jesus He could feel significant and powerful and popular by doing something foolish like throwing Himself off a mountain and watching angels rescue Him; again, Jesus quotes the truth in order to resist the pull of popularity gotten by stupid choices.

Anytime we get good things in bad ways, they aren't God's best for us. That's true with all three of these desires — physical, material, and emotional. They are the same three ways we're told not to get lured away from God in 1 John 2:15 – 17: *"Do not love the world or anything in the world. If anyone loves the world, the love of the Father is not in him. For everything in the world — the cravings of sinful man, the lust of his eyes and the boasting of what he has and does — comes not from the Father but from the world. The world and its desires pass away, but the man who does the will of God lives forever."*

Here are those same verses from *The Message* paraphrase:

"Don't love the world's ways. Don't love the world's goods. Love of the world squeezes out love for the Father. Practically everything that goes on in the world — wanting your own way,

*wanting everything for yourself, wanting to appear important—
has nothing to do with the Father. It just isolates you from him.
The world and all its wanting, wanting, wanting is on the way
out—but whoever does what God wants is set for eternity."*

That wanting, wanting, wanting is the pull with which
Satan is tempting you. Temptation of any kind is Satan's
invitation to get our needs met outside the will of God—in
an almost limitless number of ways. Seeking approval from
others, soothing loneliness by hooking up with that cute
guy, giving in to unhealthy physical desires like overeating
or starving yourself, or even wanting a new outfit, bag, or
hairstyle to make you feel new and improved ... As we will
cover in Part Two of this book, these are all examples of
ways the enemy loves to tempt us.

Satan's very name means "one who casts something
between two to cause a separation." He wants to separate
us from God. One of the subtle ways he does this is to plant
the insidious thought in our mind that God will not meet
our needs—that God is not enough. Satan wants us to feel
alone, restless, and unsatisfied, so that we turn to his offer-
ings instead.

This wanting, wanting, wanting is what pulls at Halley,
a "good girl" committed to reading her Bible first thing in
the morning, to make an exception and check her Facebook
notifications and text messages instead. Longing for attention, it makes Halley's day if someone special leaves her
a comment. If she feels ignored, her whole day is ruined.
Instead of feeling spiritually prepared to face each morning,
she's emotionally vulnerable.

It's what sends the budget-conscious Mia off on a
spending spree—just one more accessory to make her "new

and improved," like the makeover reality shows tell her she needs to be to get noticed. Mia feels the thrill of the sale in the moment. But as she's hiding the bags from her parents, shame creeps in.

It's what sends McKenna, a senior who committed herself to therapy and being healthy after a fight with bulimia, back to binging and purging. She doesn't know how else to handle her life: the hurtful comments, a stressful schedule, or demands and pressures that feel beyond her control. It seems the only thing she *can* control is what she puts into her body — and the satisfaction of that control is something she often craves more than anything. So with great justification she indulges only to have a bloated stomach. Then she purges only to have a deflated heart.

This subtle message sold to us by Satan can be exposed when we break it down to understanding the difference between a need and a want.

Your Idols

All of the examples above were wants, not needs. But, oh, how Satan wants to make them one and the same.

When the difference between *want* and *need* starts getting skewed, we start compromising. We start justifying. And it sets us up to start getting our needs met outside the will of God. When we do that, when we respond to these lies of Satan — or even just our own desires! — we're taking a craving or a "want" and turning it into an idol.

When the Bible talks about idols it isn't just talking about little stone men that ancient cultures relied on as gods. An idol is *anything* — including otherwise good things! — we are looking to or relying on other than the one true God. An idol is a "God substitute," something you are looking to, to make you happy—like a gorgeous body, an attentive boyfriend, finally having the latest and greatest cell phone, the approval of a certain group of friends, or getting into the "right" college. Those desires aren't necessarily bad, but you know you are making something an idol when you feel deprived, depressed, or even panicked at the idea of not having it. Relying on God will never make us feel this way, because only He can truly fill that hole inside of us. Relying on anything else will eventually leave us lacking, because everything else is merely temporary.

When Shaunti lived in New York City, she heard her pastor, Tim Keller, give a great illustration of how we can know whether we are making something an idol. He brought a heavy four-foot-tall pillar on the stage, and as he spoke to the congregation he casually rested his weight against the pillar, smiling, one leg crossed over the other, as if he was chatting with friends and leaning on a high-topped table in a coffee shop. After a few minutes, he asked the congregation to imagine what would happen if the pillar was suddenly taken away. It was clear that he would fall over.

He explained that an idol is anything we lean against like that; anything we are relying on to support us. We know we are making something an idol if we would topple over once it is gone. In a recent article, here's another way Tim Keller described it:

> Sin isn't only doing bad things, it is more funda-
> mentally making good things into ultimate things.
> Sin is building your life and meaning on anything,
> even a very good thing, more than on God. Whatever
> we build our life on will drive us and enslave us. Sin
> is primarily idolatry.... Making an idol out of some-

thing means giving it the love you should be giving your Creator and Sustainer.[1]

We do that with so many of our desires and wants—but when we rely on or lean on any other way of meeting our desires than our firm and immoveable God, we will eventually find those things crumbling underneath us. And at that point, we will topple over and end up with heartbreak and discontent.

I can't say this enough: Satan is a liar. The more we fill ourselves with his distorted desires, the more empty we'll feel. That's true with each of the desires mentioned above—physical, emotional, and material. The more we become overly obsessed about our wants, the more wrong desires grow and the more distant God will seem.

Remember, Satan wants to separate you from God's best plans. He wants to separate you from God's proper provision and he wants to separate you from God's peace. Rest assured God has a plan for your good and a hope for your future. He promises if you seek Him, He will lead you through life. The journey may not always be easy, but you won't be alone. Through Scripture, God says He, "will meet all your needs according to his glorious riches in Christ Jesus" (Philippians 4:19).

Unfortunately, at times it can be hard to pick out God's plans or God's will from everything else. Here's what we need to remember:

- God's provision sustains life. Satan's temptation drains life.
- God's provision satisfies the soul. Satan's temptation gratifies the flesh and often focuses on the body—sex, food, wealth, clothes, and other things in the world.

- God's provision in the short term will reap blessings in the long term. Satan's temptation in the short term will reap heartache in the long term.

Why not try filtering some of your decisions today through these truths? For example:

- Is checking your Facebook notifications and text messages first thing in the morning going to help you crave God, or attention from others?
- Is reading your Bible first thing in the morning going to help sustain your life or drain your life?
- Will this junk food you're turning to for comfort satisfy your soul or gratify your body? (Or, for those tempted to deplete their bodies of the healthy food they need, will this decision sustain your life or drain your life?)
- Will buying this new outfit that you're craving now reap blessings or heartache long term?

Oh, sweet friend, consider these realities when making choices today. Trust God. Embrace truth. Live the reality that you were made for more than a vicious cycle of craving things that can't ever really satisfy you.

God created you to crave, want, desire, think about, and long for something—for *Him*. All those feelings of desire have a place. A healthy place. You were made to be deeply satisfied by Him and Him alone.

takeaway

Satan tries to distract us from God. He wants us to get legitimate needs met in an illegitimate way.

the action plan

In your journal, try to identify a few cravings, and think through how you are meeting them right now. Is there anything you might be relying on or leaning on other than God?

To figure this out, make a list of three or four emotional, physical, or material desires that tug at you, and write down what you do to fulfill those desires. For example, if you crave the approval of friends, do you sometimes go with others to parties you know aren't healthy? If you feel empty and unhappy, do you try to feel satisfied with food — or with the feeling of power that comes from denying yourself food? If you are feeling unnoticed by guys, do you feel like a hot new outfit will get their attention? List those three or four ways you try to fulfill your desires on your own, and ask God to show you more in the days ahead.

chapter

Made for More

When I (Lysa) was a senior in high school, I was invited to a college party. I had a friend who'd graduated the year before me, and she became my favorite person in the world the day she invited me to her sorority party.

Cool doesn't even begin to describe what I felt as I and my pink jelly shoes made our way into that party. (Those were the "it" shoes of my day.) By the end of the night my friend and I were giggling over the attention given to us by two good-looking college boys. As the party died down, they invited us over to their place.

Part of me was so flattered that I wanted to go. A much bigger part of me didn't. I knew it wasn't good to get into a car with guys I didn't know—and I suspected they wanted to do more than just hang out and talk. But plans got made, and before I knew it we were getting into their car and driving away.

I was not a Christian at this point in my life. Not even close. And I certainly can't say I'd ever heard God speak to me, but in the midst of this situation, I did.

"This isn't you, Lysa. You were made for more than this."

Truth. A gift of truth, planted deep within me when God personally knit me together. Untied and presented at just the right time.

I wound up making an excuse for a quick exit and walked back to my car alone that night. I mentally beat myself up for acting like a young, immature high schooler who couldn't handle being a college party girl. But looking back, I want to stand up on a chair and clap, clap, clap for my little high-schooler self!

There were other times in my growing-up years, though, when I heard this truth loud and clear within the confines of my soul and, sadly, I refused to listen. These were the darkest years of my life. I wasn't made to live a life that dishonors the Lord.

No one is.

"You were made for more, Lysa, you were made for more."

So, what does it mean that we were made for more? It means we were made for more than to be stuck in defeating situations. We were made to live like Proverbs 3:5–6 challenges us: "Trust in the LORD with all your heart and lean not on your own understanding; in all your ways acknowledge him, and he will make your paths straight."

Here's how *The Message* interprets Proverbs 3:5–12:

> Trust God from the bottom of your heart; don't try to figure out everything on your own. Listen for God's voice in everything you do, everywhere you go; he's the one who will keep you on track.
>
> Don't assume that you know it all. Run to God! Run from evil! Your body will glow with health, your very bones will vibrate with life!

Honor God with everything you own; give him the first and the best. Your barns will burst, your wine vats will brim over. But don't, dear friend, resent God's discipline; don't sulk under his loving correction. It's the child he loves that GOD corrects; a father's delight is behind all this.

I broke these verses apart hoping you would notice the same thing I did. Once again, the Bible is addressing the three specific areas we're tackling in this book:

Emotional Desires: "Listen for God's voice." We must crave God's voice of truth over the shifting voices of friends and boys. People will accept us today and possibly reject us tomorrow. God accepts and loves those in relationship with Him today, tomorrow, and into eternity.

Here's a great verse to post on the top of your computer as a constant reminder of God's love for you: "For I am convinced that neither death nor life, neither angels nor demons, neither the present nor the future, nor any powers, neither height nor depth, nor anything else in all creation, will be able to separate us from the love of God that is in Christ Jesus our Lord" (Romans 8:38–40).

We were made for more in our emotional desires. We were made to crave God's voice.

Physical Desires: Proverbs 3 continues; "He's (God is) the one who will keep you on track. Don't assume that you know it all. Run to God! Run from evil! Your body will glow with health, your very bones will vibrate with life!" When we trust God to keep our physical desires in line with truth, we are more likely to make healthy choices for our body. For example, God made us to consume food; food was never meant to consume us. Whether food is our personal physical struggle, or something else occupies that position, we can't assume we can conquer our issues on our own.

Here's a great verse reminding us specifically how God helps heal our food issues: "They loathed all food and drew near the gates of death. Then they cried to the LORD in their trouble, and he saved them from their distress. He sent forth his word and healed them" (Psalm 107:18–20a).

He sent forth His word and He healed them. Wow. What power there is in God's truth. What hope that gives us. We must get into God's Word and let God's Word get into us.

We were made for more in our physical desires. We were made to crave God's truth.

Material Desires: "Honor God with everything you own; give him the first and the best. Your barns will burst, your wine vats will brim over." Many times we buy new things to feel improved in ourselves and to get noticed by others. Instead, ask yourself: Wouldn't it be so much better to be noticed by God as a young person who honors·God with her money and possessions?

How am I honoring God with my possessions? Am I giving back to God at least a tenth of my earnings? Or do I assume giving is what I'll do when I'm older?

We should honor God as faithful owners of that which we possess … not be possessed with that which we own. Remember what the Bible says: "For where your treasure is, there your heart will be also" (Luke 12:34).

We were made for more in our material desires. We were made to crave God's provision.

So, are we living like we are made for more?

I think everyone gets to a place sometimes where they have to honestly assess "How I am doing?" This soul-searching is not even a heart-to-heart conversation we have with a friend or family member; it's one of those middle-of-the-night contemplations where there's no one to fool. There's no glossing over the realities staring us in the face. Sometimes we know certain things need to change, but it's easier to make excuses than tackle them head-on. Rationalizations are so appealing:

> *I'm good in every other area.*
> *I make so many sacrifices already.*
> *I need this comfort right now—I'll deal with my issues later.*
> *I just can't give this up.*
> *The Bible doesn't specifically say this is wrong.*
> *It's not really a problem. If I really wanted to make a change, I could—I just don't want to right now.*
> *Oh, for heaven's sake, everyone has issues. So what if this is mine?*

And on and on and on. But excuses always get us nowhere fast. I suspect if you've read this far, these same scripts of rationalization have played out in your mind. A whole lifetime could be spent making excuses, giving in, feeling guilty, resolving to do better, mentally beating ourselves up for not sticking to what we know needs to change, feeling like a failure, and then resigning ourselves to the idea that things can't change.

I don't want to spend a lifetime in this cycle, and I suspect you don't either.

So before you put this book down and possibly give in to the unhealthy emotional, physical, or material cravings screaming inside your head, wait for just a second. Don't let go. You've already spent a few minutes headed in the right direction by picking up this book and reading this far.

Keep going. And whisper over and over, "I am made for more."

Are You Ready?

So ... are you ready to take an honest, head-on look at those things that beckon to you to believe (and act) like you *aren't* made for more? Let's take a deep breath and tackle those things that can so easily be "God substitutes" — those cravings and deep desires that aren't bad in themselves, but that we too easily rely on. Here is how we define the three cravings in this book:

- A craving to feel accepted, wanted, and loved — the "Emotional Craving"
- A craving to feel comforted by physical pleasure, beauty, and satisfaction — the "Physical Craving"
- A craving for a possession that makes you feel improved, noticed, and special — the "Material Craving"

In each of the next three chapters, Shaunti is going to take the lead as we walk through each of these deep desires. Please remember that these are desires that God *wants* to satisfy. Because in reality, each one of these is a spiritual longing — the longing of thirsty people who crave a living water that *only* God can supply.

takeaway

When you are tempted, remind yourself: " I am made for more."

the action plan

In your journal, identify at least one way that you have given into the *wrong* way of filling a craving. (It's okay—nobody but God will see your journal, and He knows the answer already.) How would remembering "I am made for more" have changed your choice and/or its outcome?

PART TWO

Searching for Satisfaction

The Emotional Craving
I want to feel loved and accepted

When I (Shaunti) was in high school, I knew a lot of cute guys. There was just one problem: I was the girl who was always the guy's "friend," the one the guys talked with long and deeply about their frustrations with their girlfriends or asked for advice about how (other) girls think. You know Taylor Swift's song "You Belong with Me," about having a secret crush on the guy with whom she's "just friends"? Yeah. Only unlike in her music video, the story didn't end with me showing up at the prom and finding that the guy was in love with me all along. In fact, I didn't even *go* to my senior prom.

Oh, I pretended I was sooo over high school and just didn't want to bother. But the hard truth is I was simply sad that I didn't have a boyfriend—had never had a real boyfriend, in fact. A few dates here and there didn't count. Deep down inside, I felt so awkward, so unsure of myself, so insecure, and I wanted someone who would sweep me off my feet and show me that I was totally worthy of being loved.

Fast forward a few years to when I'm in college, and

along comes Matt. (Names have been changed.) Matt was confident, charming, handsome; the guy that everyone gravitated toward. And he asked *me* to go out with him! I wanted someone to show me that I was loved and love*able*, and there he was, giving me all this romantic attention.

The problem was, I had no idea that I was looking to the wrong things to feel loveable. As a result, I didn't want to look too closely at Matt's "attentiveness." I didn't want to notice that my charming, handsome boyfriend tended to flirt with other girls. I didn't want to listen to my roommate when she warned me that she'd seen him with his old girlfriend. I enjoyed the tingle that shot from my brain to my toes when he kissed me, and tried to ignore my discomfort with how far he wanted to push me physically, even when I told him I was uncomfortable. And I ruthlessly banished the feelings of confusion or hurt that rose up at the derisive way he sometimes spoke to me. He was just stressed from finals, I told myself. Or my roommate must have been mistaken about what she saw. Maybe I just wasn't trying hard enough to make him happy . . .

It is amazing the number of excuses and rationalizations the average girl can come up with to justify something she knows very well is dysfunctional and wrong.

And it got even worse. I was devastated to learn that for the last semester that he was my boyfriend, he was also his old girlfriend's boyfriend. (This was pre-Facebook, of course; it's a lot harder to get away with that today!) But believe it or not, when he looked mournfully into my eyes, said "I love you so much," and begged for another chance, I took him back.

WHY would I do such a thing???

Because I was craving the feeling of being accepted and loved. Even though what I had was a complete counterfeit for *true* love, *true* acceptance, it filled at least a little bit of that hole inside of me. That is what we call the "Emotional Craving."

Have you ever been there? Whether or not you've ever put up with a two-timing boyfriend, I'll bet you know what this craving feels like.

You want to be included by people at school; being part of the group tells you that you are likeable, you fit in. It's not just that you are accepted ... you are accept-able!

You want your friends to comment on your Facebook posts, to friend you, re-tweet you, or follow your blog. If people care what you have to say, if people are paying attention, you feel special.

You want to feel the affection of a special guy who sticks with you even after he has seen the good, bad, and the ugly; it tells you that you are truly loveable and worthy of being loved.

Now, there's absolutely nothing wrong with wanting to be accepted, noticed, and loved! The issue is *how* we get that feeling met. And this is something almost every one of us needs to wrestle with, because this desire is almost universal among us females. (Guys have emotional cravings too, but they tend to be different ones.) In the extensive surveys I've conducted over the years, nine in ten girls say they have this craving.

Some of you may know that I'm a social researcher, and have spent the last ten years investigating the most private inner thoughts of men and women from teens to adults, and writing a series of books—such as *For Women Only: What You Need to Know about the Inner Lives of Men*—to help members of the opposite sex understand each other. The book for teenage guys, *For Young Men Only* (*FYMO*), is all about how teenage girls tend to think and feel. And one thing that most surprises our guy readers is that 91 percent of girls — even the most confident-looking, attractive, capable, popular girls — say they are sometimes privately insecure and question how others view them.[1]

What my fellow researchers and I have found is that the cry of almost every girl's heart (not just yours!) is "Am I loveable? Am I attractive? Am I special?"

Did you notice that within that question are the three deep cravings we're covering in this book — emotional, physical, and material? *The three cravings are, at their core, an effort to get an answer to our big heart-cry question.* And as my putting up with a two-timing boyfriend shows, we can make some pretty foolish choices when we are looking to anything other than God for the answer. In fact, in *FYMO*, here's what we told the puzzled guys:

> When you see a great girl go for "bad boy" instead of the nice guy, it's probably because the bad boy [who was willing to approach her directly] gave her the best answer to her big question … The question *every* girl is asking: *Am I attractive, special, and loveable?*[2]

In *FYMO*, we use this to help the guys understand that this private insecurity exists, so they grasp how important it is to be careful with a girl's heart. It also helps them understand why girls are so drawn toward guys who approach a girl with confidence — and why we wish the nice guys would actually be the ones to do so.

The ACTUAL Answer to the Question

Every girl—every woman too—wants the reassurance that she is loveable (and beautiful, and special, which we'll be talking about in the next two chapters). But we are making a critical mistake when we look to guys or friends or any other worldly source for that reassurance, because they can never provide the *actual* answer to our big question.

I mean, think about it: in the end, are you loveable because a guy says "I love you"? His words certainly can make you feel that way—but do they actually *make* you loveable? Of course not! And you'd be in so much trouble if they did. Because if his words had the ability to actually "make it so," what would it mean if that particular guy stopped loving you? Would it suddenly mean that you actually weren't loveable ... just because you didn't have someone's romantic affection at that particular moment in time?

What you are *really* looking for is not the temporary answer that will change based on circumstances: what you are longing for is the *actual* answer. And the only one who can give it is the One who created you, who put you together piece by piece, who knows every secret thought, everything you've ever done. It is an awesome thought that *His* answer to that deep heart-cry question—*Am I loveable? Am I worthy of being loved?*—is a shouted-from-the-rooftops *YES!*

You are a precious creation of God, lovingly crafted by the Master's hand. You need to sit at the feet of a great and glorious Father God and hear Him say, "My daughter, you are worthy of being loved—not because of the personality, charm, or sense of humor that I have given you, but *because you are so precious to me that I died for you.*"

Giving It Up to Get More

This realization, this truth, is sometimes hard to absorb — in fact, I suspect all of us will spend a lifetime learning to live in this truth. But you can make a start. You can break the cycle of looking to anything other than God to fill your emotional cravings.

Take whatever it is you fear — for example, "I'm so worried I'll be alone, that no one will ever really love me" — and give it up to the Lord with complete trust in His goodness and care for you in that area. Literally tell God that you want Him to truly be in charge of your life, and that you are willing to accept whatever that means for you — including trusting Him to fill your emotional cravings in His way.

It was through this prayer of relinquishment that I broke my reliance on the affection and acceptance of others, rather than on God. By the time I graduated from college, Matt and I had broken up, and I was so worried about being alone. I saw so many wonderful Christian women in their thirties or forties who were single, even though they deeply wanted to be married. They were refusing to compromise God's standards, they were waiting on the Lord, but they hadn't met that special someone.

In my mid-twenties, I'll admit that my heart cried out, *God, I don't want that to be me!* I'll admit that every time I met a nice Christian guy, I would wonder "Are you the one?" My emotional craving was only getting stronger, and I was looking to fill it, but with no real answer.

Then I went off to graduate school and became interested in this cute friend named Jeff. I saw the pattern all over again — I was so interested in him, but we were just friends.

I was craving more. And then one day I read a powerful article called "The Prayer of Relinquishment" by a Christian leader of many years ago, Catherine Marshall.

Marshall told of many years of illness and of begging God to heal her, but never getting the answer she wanted. Then she realized something: if He is God, and if we are really His servants, *our lives are truly not our own*. We need to "relinquish" (give up) what we so desperately want, and tell our heavenly Father that we are willing, truly willing, to give every one of our desires to Him, so He can fully use our lives for His purposes—even if sometimes the path would be quite different than the one we would have chosen.

I read that article and started sobbing. I realized I had to totally give my craving for the love and affection of a man over to God. I had to say "Thy will be done, not mine," and truly *mean* it. I got down on my knees beside the bed and held my hands out in front of me, as if I was holding all my dreams, all my hopes, all my secret longings for a man who would love me, and I said, "Here, Lord, take it. I desire a loving husband so much, but I relinquish that desire to you completely. Take it, Lord, before I take it back!"

I was emotionally wiped out, but I was filled with peace. And that peace gave me the supernatural ability to actually be okay with being "just friends" with the most amazing man I'd ever known during his entire last year of graduate school, without being anxious (well, most of the time!) that he would graduate, move away, and I'd never know "what could have been." I had that peace until the day came, six weeks before Jeff graduated, when he asked me out to lunch and told me, with a private grin, that he'd been praying for the last nine months about whether I was the woman he was supposed to marry.

I just about burst! What an amazing gift of God, to give me back what I had *truly* relinquished.

It is so very true that our lives are not our own, and God must have the right to every part of our lives. Now, it is also very true that — as I've found in many other areas — God doesn't always give us back what we sacrifice; He may see purposes and plans for our lives that we cannot yet see. And sometimes things happen in a way we don't want simply because we live in a fallen world. But the indisputable reality is that our Father *adores* us. We are loveable. We are beautiful. We are special. And He delights in giving good and wonderful things to His children.

takeaway

Every girl wonders, "Am I loveable? Am I beautiful? Am I special?" And God's shouted-from-the-rooftops answer is YES!

That doesn't mean that we always get what we think we want. But when we truly give our cravings over to Him, God's answer is usually much, much better.

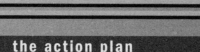

the action plan

Is there something you need to truly relinquish to God? Some dream, some want, some deep desire? Write it down in your journal, along with a prayer truly relinquishing it to Him. Ask Him to show you *His* will for your life, regardless of where that path leads. And remember that your loving Father desires good things for His children.

chapter 5

The Physical Craving
I want to feel comforted by physical satisfaction and pleasure

Let me (Shaunti) tell you about two girls I know; two sisters.

The older one, Brittany, is vivacious, has never met a stranger, and has lots of friends. The younger one, Courtney, is more reserved, quiet, and has a few deep friendships. Brittany has a short, sturdy, athletic build, which is great for blowing a powerful serve past her opponents in tennis. Courtney is tall, lithe, and graceful—perfect for the ballet that is her passion. But privately, when they look in the mirror, both girls have a problem: they are extremely insecure about how they look. And they are not handling their worry in healthy ways.

Brittany turns to food for comfort. She rationalizes that she's burning it off in tennis, or she's studied so hard she deserves those chips, but deep down, she knows she is eating because she's bored or anxious, not because she's hungry. And since she's taking in more food than her body needs, she sees her clothes size creeping up. She's not healthy. She wishes she could look like her sister, but her body type will never match that want. So she indulges and then feels shame, like she can never get it right. She's caught in a vicious cycle.

Courtney looks at her figure and sees no boobs or hips, and she hates how she looks. In addition, despite being slender, she still thinks she weighs too much. And she feels pressured by wanting to get a dance scholarship, so she secretly stops eating enough. Or she eats something and then purges. She finds herself getting faint; she's not healthy. She looks thin on the outside — in fact, she looks more and more like some of the waifs on magazine covers — but she doesn't have anything like the healthy body God designed for her. She feels anxious and depressed, and indulges in cutting. That feels good for a little while, but then she's full of shame and self-loathing, just like when she purges her meal. She's caught in a vicious cycle.

Both of these are wonderful girls with great personalities, caring hearts, and a desire to please God with their lives. Both have been given unique and beautiful physical characteristics and talents. But despite that, both are unhappy.

Why? Because both these godly young women are looking to physical satisfaction to give them a sense of pleasure that only God can satisfy. And despite being very disciplined in some areas (Brittany in tennis, Courtney in ballet), both are being undisciplined and unhealthy with their physical cravings. For example, they are using food in ways God never intended. They are trying to fill a legitimate craving in illegitimate ways.

In the limited space of this chapter, we are primarily going to be focusing on how easy it is for any of us to seek satisfaction in how we look, or in what we do or don't eat, but clearly there are many other ways (alcohol, drugs, cutting …) we might seek to fill that void.

And each time we seek satisfaction in "something else," we — like Brittany and Courtney — are actually scorning the unique make up God chose for us.

"I Just Wanted to Be Beautiful."

In the 2010 movie *The Chronicles of Narnia: The Voyage of the Dawn Treader*,[1] based on the book by C. S. Lewis, teenage Lucy Pevensie secretly longs to look more like her beautiful older sister, Susan. She is tempted by the existence of a spell that promises to make her "the beauty you've always wanted to be," and eventually recites the incantation. In a dreamlike state, she sees herself morphing into Susan. But she suddenly finds that once she turns into Susan, her family has never heard of Lucy. She has vanished out of existence. Terrified, she jerks awake and sees that Aslan — the great lion who represents Jesus — is there with her.

"What have you done, child?" he asks.

She tries to explain why she gave in to her craving, concluding, "I just wanted to be beautiful, like Susan. That's all."

But then Aslan shows her just how big a deal that actually was: "You wished yourself away. And with it, so much more." He reminds her that if she hadn't existed, her family would never know of Narnia.

Gently but firmly, the great Lion says, "You doubt your value. Don't run from who you are."

Lucy is contrite. She gets it. She decides to be pleased with what Aslan says about her rather than continuing to look in the wrong places to feel satisfied. And some time later, when an admiring young girl tells her, "When I grow up, I want to be just like you," Lucy sits down with her, looks her in the eyes, and says, "When you grow up, you should be just like *you*."

In this movie, Lucy has learned the vital lesson that we all must learn in the face of our craving for satisfaction or pleasure in physical things — whether that is seeking solace in trying to get down to a certain clothes size, in being reassured of our looks, in food, drugs, or alcohol, in cutting, or any other worldly source. Satisfying that worldly craving will leave us filled for only a very short time, and then it will leave us empty and regretful. This is especially true since, by definition, so many of the ways we fill physical cravings tend to be physically self-destructive.

The Myth that Looks Real

Why is it so easy to give in to that temptation to engage in self-destructive behavior, like eating more than our body actually needs, eating less than our body needs, beating ourselves up over our looks, seeking temporary pleasure in alcohol or drugs, or secretly cutting? Especially, why is it so easy when we've done it before and *know* it will feel good for only a short time, and then it'll feel terrible?

Similarly, why is it so easy to compare ourselves with others? In a focus group we conducted with teenage girls about these topics, several girls nodded when one seventeen-year-old girl, Tia, said, "When I am by myself, I think I look fine until someone else walks in. It's different when you are by yourself than when you are with others. The problem comes up because there are so many others who look so good! Magazines, movies, TV—even girls we interact with every day cause problems. That's when you start to feel bad about yourself. You were okay until you started comparing."

It is vital to remember that there is an unseen enemy who is weaving a web of lies to tempt us to self-destruction, to comparison, and those lies sound so good in the moment. They are handcrafted to hit *your* weaknesses.

Do any of these sound familiar?

You look at the cover of a magazine and think, *I should be able to look like that.*

You feel depressed because your boyfriend suddenly isn't returning your calls, so you think, *Those cookies will make me feel better.*

You feel anxious about your weight, so you think, *The best thing to do is to just not eat.*

Lies—every one of them. The Evil One creates a myth that he holds up as real—and then beats you up when you don't meet that impossible standard! See how cruel he is? And how insane it is to give in to that?

The two sisters I mentioned earlier, Brittany and Courtney, were listening to those lies, and an unhealthy search for pleasure through food and body image was consuming them. If we're not careful, every one of us can follow the same lie. Remember: we were made to consume food; obsession with food (whether that means too much or too little) was never supposed to consume us.

So What *Was* Food Made For?

In the Bible, God seems to lay out three main ways we are to use food:

- Daily as fuel for our bodies
- Occasionally as part of the enjoyment of a public celebration (such as a wedding feast)
- Occasionally (by giving it up) as part of the discipline of fasting and prayer

One of my friends who is significantly overweight was recently told by his doctor, "You will never lose weight until you stop being in love with food and begin to think of food as simply fuel for your body. You put in as much as you need to run your engine. That's when you will be healthy."

That's a pretty good summary, but I also think it's not enough—I've seen personally that even when I am trying to eat "just enough," I can completely sabotage myself and gain weight simply because I don't know how my body handles certain types of food. (For example, did you know that to our bodies there's almost no difference between a plain baked potato, a piece of white bread, and a piece of birthday cake? If I'm going to cheat, I'd rather *know* that I'm cheating—and have the birthday cake! We have written up a short, informal summary for you that you might find helpful, titled, "How your body handles food." You can find it on *madetocrave.org/youngwomen* under "freebies.")

The Bible shows us that God created food in order to run our bodies and keep us healthy—no more or less. And the Bible also describes our body as a temple in which God dwells. So depriving our body in extreme or unhealthy ways in order to hit a certain weight, or overeating in order to feel better, is a bit like carving out a little wooden idol of a god, placing it in a church, and bowing down to worship it. It's insulting to God and dangerous to you.

In fact, eating in extreme excess of what our bodies need is considered gluttony, which is warned against like lying, drunkenness, or any other sin that separates us from God. For example: "Be not among drunkards or among gluttonous eaters of meat, for the drunkard and the glutton will come to poverty, and slumber will clothe them with rags" (Proverbs 23:20 – 21, ESV). And similarly, we see a strong warning against denying ourselves in extreme ways as well. "Some became fools through their rebellious ways and suffered affliction because of their iniquities. They loathed all food and drew near the gates of death" (Psalm 107:17 – 18).

Thankfully, despite those clear warnings against either type of excess, there's nothing in the Bible that suggests we are to deny ourselves all pleasure from food: God clearly made food to taste good to us, and we are told that there will be feasting in heaven!

In fact, imagining heaven will give us a sense for how we might make healthy choices when faced with physical cravings. When you want to go back for a second helping of dessert or ignore your hunger; when you want to stand in front of the mirror and mentally pick apart all your flaws, or secretly binge and purge, ask yourself: If I were in heaven, would I do this thing? Often, we realize, no, I wouldn't — because there would be no need to!

And that gives us a great example of what it means to satisfy our cravings with God. Because in heaven, we will be so saturated with pleasure and satisfaction in the presence of the Lord that we will simply have no *desire* to eat more—or less—than we need. We will feel no need to stand in front of the mirror and worry about whether we look thin enough, or tall enough, or pretty enough. We will feel no compulsion to give in to any of our earthly physical cravings. We will be in God's presence, and none of the old cravings will have a hold on us because they will already be filled by Him alone.

takeaway

Don't wish yourself away. "When you grow up, you should be just like you."

the action plan

In your journal, write one or more physical cravings that tend to tempt you. (Like comparing your figure with others, eating less than or more than your body needs, purging, cutting, and so on.) Leave a blank space by each.

In the next few days, when you next encounter that craving, ask yourself "If I were in heaven, would I do this thing?" Pray and ask God for strength to resist the worldly temptation at that moment. Also, ask Him for the strength to tell someone about what you're going through, so it is not hidden. Then go back to your journal and write what you did and what the outcome was.

chapter  6

The Material Craving
I want something that makes me feel special, improved, and new

I (Shaunti) want you to imagine that it's a Saturday, you have a free day, a good friend by your side, and a $200 gift card in your pocket from Grandma. (Yeah, I know, that's a lotta love from Grandma, but work with me here.) You're wandering through a beautiful shopping area, looking at clothes, the spa, the makeup counter ... and a few hours later, you walk out with a cute new outfit, great shoes, two new shades of lip gloss, and a funky bag that you just love. You feel awesome, right?

WHY?

It's not so much that you have acquired $192.97 worth of new stuff ... No, that's not it. It's not just that you've got a new favorite pair of shoes (although that is certainly quite cool). It's that you feel ... *improved*. You feel special. New. You can't wait to oh-so-casually wear your new outfit on Monday at school and turn some heads. It's quite a high.

There's almost a feeling of power.

Many of us experience a deep desire for something that will make us feel that way. And that is what we mean by the Material Craving. I have asked many girls, "Do you know how you feel when you get a new outfit?" And every girl grins and nods her head. I have never gotten a blank look. Everyone knows what I'm talking about.

When you see the words "material craving," you may think, *That's not my issue. I'm not materialistic. I'm not in love with money.* Well, what we call the "material craving" is *not* the same thing as being in love with money or wanting to accumulate more and more stuff. No ... the material craving we are talking about is far more sneaky. Sneaky enough that Satan can easily tempt us with it, without us even realizing we're looking to something material to meet a deep emotional need! And certainly without us realizing that we're turning our backs on God in the process.

As with all the cravings we're talking about, it's not necessarily wrong to want to feel noticed or special. It's not necessarily wrong to love wandering the stores and finding cool clothes, the latest gadgets, or a pair of shoes that makes you really happy. I take Jesus very literally when He says that God delights in giving good things to His children.

The question we have to ask ourselves is *why* we want to go wander the stores or go get that manicure. Is it because we want to give ourselves a treat and enjoy the day with a friend? Or is because we're just feeling "blah" about ourselves, our friends, or our life and we want something that will make us feel better? Or, even more to the point, is it because we're depressed that we didn't make the cheerleading squad (or debate team, or get the job we wanted, or whatever ...) and "retail therapy" is the quickest cure?

We have to be really careful that we're not using shopping in the same way someone else would use drugs or alcohol—to give a lift, or to temporarily numb the pain and make it all go away for a while. Because if that's what is going on, then—as you can guess by now—you will simply find yourself back in the same position in a few days. A temporary fix is just a temporary fix.

Even worse is the irony that, as we follow our craving to acquire something that will make us feel unique and special, we all too often try to follow the crowd in order to feel that way. We want to feel unique, but then what we buy (the cute outfit, the great shoes) is often what will make us look like everyone else and fit in with everyone else. It's *not* what will be unique and special.

As you can imagine, attempting to feel special by trying to fit in with others (instead of seeking that reassurance from God) will leave us feeling even emptier when we succeed. We seek uniqueness and ended up feeling the opposite—among other people who, underneath their polished, stylish, shop-'til-you-drop exteriors, have the same desperate unmet need as we do.

"I Like to be Able to Look in the Mirror and Feel Confident."

In one focus group, as we talked about this desire to get something that will make us feel great, a high school senior spoke for many of the girls. "Some have new clothes and get ready in order to look good for others. Yeah, we all like that. But even before anyone sees me, I like to be able to look in the mirror and feel confident. I want to look in the mirror and say I look pretty. It feels good. It feels really good. You carry yourself with more confidence, because you *feel* confident."

Now, I like looking in the mirror and saying "I look pretty" too. (Just so you know, we never outgrow that!) And I appreciate an outfit that fits in with the current fashion as much as anyone — in fact, I wish I could be a little more like those who make it look so easy. There's nothing wrong with enjoying all of that. But it is yet another example of where we can so easily go astray if we are *relying* on that — relying on anything other than God — to give us that wonderful feeling of reassurance and confidence.

So when you're depressed because your friends said something mean, or your parents are fighting, or you're completely bummed about your grades, instead of starting with retail therapy, *go to God first*. Pour out your heart, listen to Him and what *He* says about you; how special you are, how much *He* notices you, and how, in His timing, others will too. Not so they can praise you, but so that your life can bring glory to Him.

Hear us on this: After you've talked with the Lord, there may not be *anything* wrong with you calling a friend and getting together to wander the stores and talk. But do it out of the fullness of your heart, a heart that has been filled up by God first, not out of your lack.

One way to keep this particular desire in balance comes from the way God says we are to manage our money — since, even if we do it with the correct intentions, we usually have to spend money in order to acquire something that makes us feel new and improved. The Bible says that we are to give at least 10 percent to God by tithing at church (*tithe* means *tenth*) and being generous with those in need. We are to be wise and save for the future. And we are to spend wisely within our means — never living in debt to the credit card lenders. God talks a lot about being wise with money in Scripture, because He knows that "where your treasure is, there your heart will be also" (Matthew 6:21). Obeying Him about money is one key way of keeping our hearts safe and submitting our material cravings to Him.

A Filled-up Heart

In the end, though, there is only one way that your heart can truly get the feeling you are craving, that feeling of being special and noticed. And it comes from knowing who you are: an all-important daughter of the King.

There's a scene in the 1999 movie *Anna and the King* that, for me, perfectly captures what this reality looks like. In this true story (this movie and the Broadway musical *The King and I* are both based on actual events), an 1860s British schoolteacher (played by Jodie Foster) becomes the instructor to the many children of the king of Siam (Chow Yun-Fat). Like many monarchs in his day, he is proud, stern, and all-powerful, and those around him literally prostrate themselves whenever he walks by, kneeling and pressing their faces to the floor. He's impatient as well, and his wrath pours out on anyone who interrupts or displeases him — *especially* in the formal sanctity of his throne room. Anna is nearly killed when she first dares to approach him without permission.

One day, though, the king is holding court in the throne room and someone blithely interrupts, pushing open the door and running past the hundreds of men who are quaking, prostrate, on the floor before the throne. The interloper hurries down the imposing, long aisle of the throne room and confidently pushes right past the current supplicants who are kneeling before the throne, explaining some important diplomatic business. Their voices die away at the interruption, as small feet pitter-patter up the tall stairs to the throne. And a little girl, about six years old, leans in to whisper something into the king's ear.

He immediately stops his business, stands, picks her up, and heads out the door on a mission, leaving hundreds of astonished court watchers wondering what just happened.

So ... what *did* happen? Well, the girl was his daughter. And she had the confidence to hurtle into the throne room of the king with news that was important to her (her brother was in a fight), because she knew who she was — and who her daddy was.

Just like that little girl in Siam one hundred fifty years ago, the book of Hebrews tells us we can "approach the throne of grace with confidence" (4:16) — because we are redeemed children of our mighty God.

Now take a moment and realize what that means. If we are really the children of the One who created everything that ever was and ever will be ... who set the stars in motion with just a word of His power ... who one day will come riding on the clouds of heaven to judge the whole world ... we need to seek for no other significance, no other importance, no other specialness. *We are daughters of the King!!* And He notices every single thing that we do, with an intensity that is beyond our comprehension.

The material craving is all about the old being made new: the old "blahs," the old hurts, the old concerns, the old habits, the old worries—the old reliance on yourself rather than on Him. But the Bible says that "anyone who belongs to Christ has become a new person. The old life is gone; a new life has begun!" (2 Corinthians 5:17, NLT).

We have only to ask, to not only *feel* new but to *be* new! A new pair of shoes can't do it, nor can a new haircut, that great jacket you got on sale, or a new car. Jesus is the only one who can take everything about us (all the "old" that just doesn't feel so good), redeem it, transform it, and make it new.

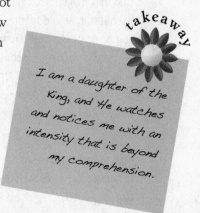

takeaway

I am a daughter of the King, and He watches and notices me with an intensity that is beyond my comprehension.

the action plan

How can your choices in managing your money acknowledge your status as a daughter of the King? Is there something you need to change? Do you need to begin tithing (giving 10 percent of) your income to your church? How can you help someone in need? Or perhaps you tithe well, but you aren't wise about your spending choices and you throw away money you really should be saving for some future need.

Also, are you aware of any areas in which you are looking to something other than God to make you feel special, new, and improved?

Ask God to show you any areas you need to focus on, and write those in your journal today. Specifically, write down exactly what you are going to do differently in the immediate weeks ahead. Then do those things, and record them in your journal, along with any thoughts or prayers about what happens as a result.

chapter

Four Reality Checks

Building a life is a lot like building a house. Just recently I (Lysa) went to see a friend's house being built. As I drove up, the outside looked almost completed — like she should be able to move in. However, when she opened the front door, there were only studs where walls would eventually be; there were only wires where light fixtures and a ceiling would be placed; and there was only cement where the flooring would be laid. Just think if my friend had decided to move in just by looking at the outside. Yes, building a life is a lot like building a house. You'd better get inside and take a look around before you decide to accept everything and move in.

Just like that house that looked good on the outside but disappointing on the inside, there are many things the world offers that may look good from the outside but won't satisfy the deep longings of our hearts. We become consumers of the world, and if we're not careful, the world can consume us, leading us away from God's best for us.

In the Bible, God tells us we must be "transformed by the renewing of our minds." In other words, we have to stop listening to the lies that are so easy to believe and get truth into our brains instead. Truth helps us see reality in the midst of many false assumptions.

The cool thing about knowing God's truth is that it's a constant reflection of God's heart. It's real. It's satisfying. It's consistent. It never shifts or changes. But to understand God's heart, we need to read the Bible and see the whole truth about the world's façades. We call these reality checks. We must have our eyes opened so we can understand that those worldly ideas aren't always as shiny and perfect and attractive as they seem from the outside.

So, let's spend a few minutes "looking inside" with a few vital reality checks about those things that we sometimes crave, which we've been covering in previous chapters.

Reality Check #1:

Even the most beautiful women struggle with body image. No matter how you try, there is unlikely to be a time when you feel "beautiful enough" to be satisfied.

I (Shaunti) am guessing that some of you are like me in that even when I am at my most fit and healthy, I struggle with how I look. I have boobs and hips, and my ancestry and heritage has given me a body type that is never going to be teeny, which I seem to see as the body type that would make me feel "beautiful enough." To make it worse, my family has spent a lot of time living and traveling overseas in an area that seems to be populated entirely by beautiful, reed-thin people, and let me tell you, when you are insecure about your figure it is really annoying to spend all your time around those women, you know?

So I was shocked when I found out they are insecure too!

A couple of years ago, the government of one of those countries asked my husband and me to conduct some workshops on our surprising findings about how men and women think. They heavily promoted the workshops through the radio program of one of the nation's most popular DJs — a charismatic, beautiful woman in her thirties who always looked stunning in the latest fashions. I was a healthy weight, but I felt fat and frumpy just standing next to her.

But then something unexpected happened. Jeff and I were on the air in her broadcast studio explaining our finding that even secure women in great relationships need to know that their husband or boyfriend finds them beautiful. A moment later, when we were on a commercial break and talking privately, the DJ wistfully told us, "That's so true. I can't hear that enough. Especially because of my flatter facial features. Whereas the dimensions of your face are so beautiful." I must have made an inadvertent noise of astonishment, because she rushed to continue. "It is so hard to come to terms with my face. You have such distinctive face bones, such distinct features. I really struggle with my flat, featureless face." She sighed. "I wish I looked more like you."

I was stunned and convicted. Stunned because I had been sitting there thinking she was so, so pretty. Convicted because the one thing she didn't like about herself was clouding her ability to see what I saw: her absolute beauty.

There, in front of me, was the reality that there is no fairy-tale point at which we'll be satisfied with how we look. We must decide to get that satisfaction from God alone.

Reality Check #2:

It is impossible to look like the images of the beautiful women in the magazines, because those images are often fake.

You may secretly think you should be able to look like those beautiful, thin women in the magazines, on the Internet, or on television. But the dirty little secret of the glamour industry is that those women actually don't and *can't* look like that: you're being tricked into comparing yourself to a standard that doesn't exist.

Nearly all of the still images that we see in the glamour industry (fashion magazines, shopping websites, billboard ads, etc.) have been airbrushed and Photoshopped to remove all blemishes, facial lines, and so-called body "flaws," and to make the women look thinner. Even some of the actresses that we see in the movies are "fixed" via computer-generated special effects. In other words, there is physically no way that most of those women could look like that in real life. And that doesn't even count the in-person touch-ups worked by the professional Hollywood makeup and lighting people, who can turn any awkward duckling into a swan for a one-hour photo shoot. (For an example of that, look up the Dove "Evolution" video on YouTube. You can also see it at *www.madetocrave.org./youngwomen*)

In the online discussion guide related to Vicki Courtney's book *Five Conversations You Must Have with Your Daughter*, she discusses a video narrated by a Diet.com spokesmodel about the Photoshop photo shoot process that is now standard in the glamour industry. (It is also on *www.madetocrave.org*.) In the video, "The Photoshop Effect," we see how the photographer takes a picture of the model in her bikini and then does the "usual" alterations to the picture, trimming in her waistline, her thighs, her arms, and so on. The photographer says, "If you trained full time as a pro athlete with trainers, and ate the way you were supposed to eat, your body could probably get close [to this Photoshopped picture], but who has time? So I do it for you."

The spokesmodel then reveals that due to her contract with Diet.com, she *does* have an extremely rigorous workout schedule, because she has to film so many exercise videos! She works her tail off and yet could never look like her own picture. In other words, the image the Photoshop expert was creating of her was physically impossible for her to attain.

Too many girls want to look like those images — have a *craving* to look like those images — never realizing that the images are fake, and looking like those women is impossible.

Reality Check #3:
That "perfection" you think you need is not what guys want anyway.

Many girls have another concern that stems from our emotional cravings as well: the images may be fake, but isn't that what all the cute guys are looking for? Having interviewed and surveyed more than a thousand teenage guys over the years, I can tell you that the answer is no: the vast majority don't expect girls to look like that and can be attracted to lots of different body types.

Let me prove it to you. For the book *For Young Women Only,* my coauthor Lisa Rice and I hired a survey company to conduct a nationally representative survey of teenage guys to find out how they privately think. It was anonymous, so the guys could be completely honest. Here's what we asked:

"TV and magazines glamorize a particular kind of girl that everyone seems to agree is hot. Despite this image, do you find yourself attracted to other kinds of girls, such as any of the following?"

- the pretty but unglamorous "girl next door"
- the "plain Jane" who is a fantastic athlete
- the sweet girl that never made an enemy
- the stocky girl with a hilarious sense of humor

And here's what they answered:

a. No. I'm only attracted to the hot *Sports Illustrated* babe.   11%
b. Yes. I find myself attracted to a variety of types of girls.   89%[1]

On this very expensive, very reliable scientific survey, almost nine out of ten teen guys say they can be attracted to all different types of girls! And in our in-person interviews, almost *every* guy we talked to said they wished girls wouldn't be so hard on themselves. While it is indeed important to them that a girl respects herself enough to make the effort to be healthy, the guys say they love girls' individuality.

All those little things that bug us (my boobs are too small, my waist is too wide, my nose is too crooked) are usually things the guys don't even notice. And they wish girls would stop thinking that guys expect all girls to look like some supermodel. When I speak at school assemblies, I play video after video of guys saying things like this comment from one high school junior:

"When it comes to appearances, just turn off the TV and throw the magazines away. Because it's not true. Guys do not like skinny girls that they can break when they give them a hug. We like girls that are just themselves, okay? Don't go on diets, don't starve yourself. Just be yourself and guys will like you for who you are."

Reality Check #4:

Since we are living in an imperfect, fallen world, there is nothing of the world that will ever make you feel new or special "enough."

The big Hollywood movie stars and professional athletes probably are the foremost experts of our time on the fact that all the "stuff" that gets you noticed doesn't, in the end, succeed in what you might think it will do, which is make you feel better about yourself. Every movie star or famous athlete gets baskets of swag filled with the newest clothes or sports shoes, the most fashionable gadgets, the most popular perfumes or makeup. World-class jewelers fall over themselves to ask the population of the red carpet to wear their latest glittering creations. What a rush! All the attention on the new gown! Being noticed by millions!

But when the paparazzi pack up and go home for the night, and the stars carefully take off their gowns and diamonds and crawl into bed, they have just as many private insecurities and as much brokenness as the rest of us. Even having the most-extreme examples of high-end, new-and-improved *stuff* do not succeed in getting these stars to some mythical state where they finally, finally feel noticed and special and satisfied "enough."

That is because each human being is geared, inside, to

be searching for a state of newness that doesn't exist in our imperfect, fallen world. It only exists in the world to come, where all sin and imperfection is wiped away.

In this world, if we set our heart on acquiring something to fill us, enough will never be enough. You don't get any better examples of that fact than when wealthy, popular, "noticed" stars like Lindsay Lohan or Winona Rider are caught stealing. These girls gave the appearance of having it all and yet wound up in jail, on drugs, in treatment facilities, and so on. They had it all—the fame, fortune, career success, glitz and glamour—yet their actions showed that on the inside they felt extreme emptiness.

This is why we must set our hearts on things above, not on earthly things. Allow yourself to be "transformed by the renewing of your mind." Don't give in to the notion that in a fallen world the things of this world will ever truly satisfy.

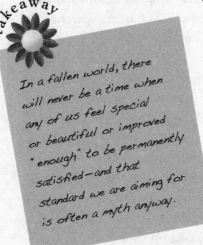

takeaway

In a fallen world, there will never be a time when any of us feel special or beautiful or improved "enough" to be permanently satisfied—and that standard we are aiming for is often a myth anyway.

the action plan

Watch the two short videos we mention in Reality Check #2. What do you think about what you saw? Write yourself a letter in your journal that you can use later, to remind yourself of what you learned from watching.

Then, think about your own assumptions. Which reality checks do you most need to absorb? Write those in your journal as well, and keep an eye out in the days and weeks ahead for the truth behind the lie that might otherwise blind you.

PART THREE

The One Craving That
Won't Leave You Empty

Growing Closer to God

I n the previous chapters we focused on how we need to rely on God to meet the deepest cravings of our heart. We also explored some good reality checks to consider. But what do we do when worldly things seem so close and God feels far away?

That bag of chocolate is in the pantry. The cell phone in my purse means I can have text conversations with friends and boys pretty instantaneously. And my favorite store — the one that just got some new shoes in stock — well, it's only a short drive from my house or, better yet, a few clicks of my mouse away.

Those things seem close.

But God? How can we really get close to Him?

We found it interesting that when we asked the girls in our focus group if they believed God could meet their needs, everyone said yes. But when we asked "how?" everyone remained silent. One girl eventually broke the tense silence by uttering, "I know God *can* meet my needs. I just don't know *how* to truly get closer to God and get these needs met by Him." Many girls nodded in agreement.

How? It's definitely a question worth dedicating this whole chapter to answering. But first, let me (Lysa) share a bit about the hard route I had to take to find this answer.

The Way of Sacrifice

Have you ever been in a situation where you vulnerably share your heart only to have someone slam your intentions and make you feel foolish? I was once at a conference doing a question and answer session when someone asked me, "How do you grow close to God?"

Great question. Possible answers swirled about in my mind. I didn't want to give a trite answer complete with the typical checklist: Go to church. Don't cuss. Read the Bible. Pray. Give to the poor.

Those are all great things, and I believe doing them pleases God. But simply checking those things off a list and then sitting back waiting for closeness to God to come won't happen. God can't be reduced to a checklist.

Growing closer to God is a whole lot less about any action we might take and a whole lot more about positioning our heart toward His. It's what I call intentionally positioning ourselves to experience God—and the posture of that position might surprise most well-meaning Christ seekers and followers.

The posture isn't standing with our arms up high or our hands outstretched. The posture is the lowest possible position we can put ourselves in: empty hands and eager hearts.

In other words, we need to communicate with our intentions, our attitude, and even our body language that He is

God, and we are not — and that we are willing to deny ourselves and give ourselves up to Him.

So, back to that question I was asked: "How do you grow close to God?"

I answered, "By making the choice to deny ourselves something that is permissible but not beneficial. And making this intentional sacrifice for the sole purpose of growing closer to God, and stripping ourselves of anything that could turn our heart from Him. After all, Jesus Himself said, 'If anyone would come after me, he must deny himself and take up his cross daily and follow me'" (Luke 9:23).

I went on to briefly explain how over the years I had felt a burning desire to become more than just a checklist Christian. Jesus says, "If anyone would come after me," which means being a disciple, growing closer to Him. Therefore, His answer of denying ourselves and taking up our cross daily, or choosing to sacrifice things that turn our hearts, is the key to following Him passionately and wholeheartedly.

I went on to tell about how right now I'm intentionally sacrificing sugar and processed foods that turn into sugar in my body once consumed. Yes, I am doing it to get healthy. But there is something much deeper going on — the deeper spiritual reasons of choosing to purify myself spiritually and learning to satisfy my longings with God, not food. And that process is daily, hourly, helping me grow closer to God.

My answer was real, vulnerable, and honest. Maybe a little too honest. The women in the audience gasped when I said I'm in a season of sacrificing sugar. It wasn't two seconds before a conference attendee grabbed the audience microphone and blurted out, "Well, if Jesus called Himself the bread of life, I can't see how sugar and processed carbs are bad at all!"

The audience erupted with laughter.

I made myself smile while feeling smaller than an ant. No, I take that back. Smaller than a wart on the end of an ant's nose. And that's pretty small.

They didn't get it.

Or maybe I didn't get it. Was I just a foolish Jesus-chasing girl with misplaced desires to please Him? Sugar for me had become like a drug. I thought about it more than I thought about God. But was I foolish to somehow think denying myself this would help me grow closer to Him?

No, I realized, I wasn't. But I was fighting against a tide of a culture — even in church! — that didn't understand the need to deny ourselves anything.

More than getting physically healthy, I wanted to get spiritually healthy. My poor outward choices were simply a manifestation of a broken spiritual condition. I knew I had to deal with the "inner me," and that meant sacrificing the thing that was keeping me captive.

Anyone struggling with a craving that is holding her captive will eventually need to come to the same conclusion. The girl who is struggling with checking her Twitter feed before checking the Bible first thing in the morning might need to fast from social media for a while. Or someone in debt might sacrifice going to the mall for a while. Often, there is simply no other way to break that hold than to give something up.

Tapping into the Holy Spirit for Self-Control

But, thankfully, this journey of growing closer to God is about so much more than just sacrifice. It really is about learning to make wiser choices daily. I'm trying. And somehow becoming a person of self-discipline honors God and helps me acquire the godly characteristic of self-control.

Galatians 5:22 tells us that the fruit of the Spirit (the evidence of God's spirit being in you) is a list of godly characteristics: love, joy, peace, patience, kindness, goodness, faithfulness, gentleness, and self-control. In the end, pursuing self-control helps my heart feel closer to Jesus and more pure to receive what He wants for me each day, instead of being clogged with guilty feelings about my poor choices.

But self-control is hard. We don't like to deny ourselves. We don't think it's necessary. We make excuses and declare, "That's nice for you, but I could never give that up." And if we're relying on ourselves, that's true. But there's another level to self-control that too few of us find.

Before the fruit of the Spirit is listed in Galatians 5:22, verse 16 reveals a power available to us that goes way beyond relying on our own strength to practice self-control: "So I say, live by the Spirit, and you will not gratify the desires of the sinful nature." In other words, live with the willingness to walk away when the Holy Spirit nudges you and says, "That's not God's best for you. That won't lead you closer to God; it will distract you from God."

Of course, the obvious question is: how can we tune into these nudges of the Holy Spirit? How can we, as verse 16 says, "live by the Spirit"?

Well, first, and most important, we have to know God and thus have His Spirit living in us. Jesus, after all, made a sacrifice far more painful and powerful than anything we will have to make when He was willing to give up His life for ours — even though we certainly did not deserve it. I love how Shaunti's pastor from New York, Tim Keller, famously summarizes the gospel. He says the essence of the gospel — the Good News — is that we are more sinful and lost than we ever dared believe, but we are more loved and forgiven than we ever dared hope.

And God says that every person must decide whether they are going to in turn accept what He did for each of us and give our lives over to Him.

Some of you may realize that you know *about* God but you don't really *know* God personally, because you've never given God your life. If not, take a moment and do that now. Use this prayer below as a guide, but don't get all caught up in trying to pray the prayer with fancy words. Talk to God. Pour out your heart to Him. He's right there with you, eager to hear what you have to say.

> *Lord, I confess that I have sinned against You and I ask You to forgive me. I am sorry that my sin has hurt You and other people in my life. I acknowledge that I could never earn salvation by my good works, but I come to You and trust in what Jesus did for me on the cross. I believe that You love me and that Jesus died and rose again so that I can be forgiven and come to know You. I ask You to come into my heart and that You would be Lord of my life. I trust You with my life and I thank You for loving me so much that I can know You here on earth, and spend the rest of eternity with You in heaven. In Jesus's name, Amen.*

If you have just given your life over to God, welcome into the family of Christ! More important than any other action now is to find a good, Bible-teaching church that will help you understand what it means to live as a follower of Jesus. Most churches have youth and young adult programs; it will be important to plug into a program that can help you learn and grow. Speaking of growing, let's return to a key way we grow closer to God, which is to "live by the Spirit." To do that, we have to know where the Spirit is and what He gives us. Amazingly, the Bible says that if we know Jesus as our personal Savior, we already have the Holy Spirit living in us!

Romans 8:11 says that the Spirit is not only living in us, but is actively giving us power to our lives that is beyond what we could possibly muster up on our own.

Now then, how do we live by this Spirit and heed His voice of wisdom and caution? Galatians 5:25 says, "Since we live by the Spirit, let us keep in step with the Spirit." In other words, we should be reading the Bible with the intention of putting into practice what we read, while asking the Holy Spirit to direct us in knowing how to do this.

I will often pray, "I need wisdom to make wise choices. I need insight to remember the words I've read in Scripture. I need power beyond what I can find on my own."

Wait.

Don't rush past that prayer. Read it again. Maybe even copy it down and make a point to pray it each day this week.

It's not a magic prayer. I still have to make the choice to walk away from the source of my temptation. And making this choice is sometimes really hard.

Eve versus the Starbucks Bakery Case

Like when I'm in line at Starbucks. The barista takes my coffee order and then waves her hand like an enticing wand, directing my attention to a case full of the delights that make a girl's taste buds dance. Seriously dance. Like the rumba, tango, and a snappy little quick step all in a row. My taste buds dance around while begging like a small child in the candy aisle.

"Would you like something?" she says.

Of course I'd like something. I'd like two or three somethings. And I'll be completely honest, it's in moments like this that I just want to ask Eve if the word *fruit* got lost in translation, and what was really dangling from that limb all those years ago were treats like this. I'm just saying.

Like I said, it's not easy. It's not easy relying on the Holy Spirit to direct us into wise choices. It's not easy to dare to actually live a life where we put Scripture to action. Especially Scriptures about self-control. It's not easy, but it is possible. Crucial, actually, if we want to grow closer to God. Remember, growing closer to God means distancing ourselves from things that distract us from Him.

Maybe you've heard of the verse that says, "With man this is impossible, but with God all things are possible" (Matthew 19:26).

I love this verse. But it is especially important to keep it in the context of where it's found in the Bible in order to really understand what's being addressed. In Matthew 19, Jesus talked to a rich young man who informed Him he was following all the rules, but still felt something was missing in his pursuit of God.

Matthew 19:20: " 'All of these [rules] I have kept,' the young man said. 'What do I still lack?' "

I doubt Mick Jagger got his inspiration from this story, but this young man's desperate question sure does remind me of the Rolling Stones' wildly popular song: "I can't get no satisfaction ... no, no, no."

Unsatisfied.

Lacking.

Incomplete.

Hollow.

Shallow.

What do I still lack?

How do I really get close to God?

Such a vulnerable question. Such a relatable question.

In verse 21, Jesus answers, "If you want to be perfect [whole], go, sell your possessions and give to the poor, and you will have treasure in heaven. Then come, follow me."

The rich young man then goes away sad, because he couldn't give up that which consumed him. He was so full with his riches he couldn't see how undernourished his soul was. Like a person who fills herself up with doughnuts to the point she refuses the healthier options of eggs and fruit, then complains of her splitting headache from the crash of the sugar high but refuses to consider giving up her doughnuts.

I might have had a little personal experience once or twice in my past sugar-filled life that led me to think of that frail little analogy.

Anyhow. Please, please notice what Jesus's direction for the denial was. *We are to deny to more closely follow.* If your struggle is overeating—like the one I described above— you're not supposed to now deny yourself food eaten for the purpose of nourishment. We need food to sustain our life! But we don't need unhealthy choices that compromise our health and keep us feeling sluggish physically and spiritually. Similarly, if your struggle is a craving for the acceptance of friends, you shouldn't deny yourself friends just because you have a tendency to rely on them for your self-image. Rather, you should practice denying yourself those actions, patterns, and perhaps times with certain specific people that pull you away from God and *His* affirmation for your life.

Notice that with this rich young man, Jesus didn't say, "Give away your money and live as a homeless person." No, He said, "Give up the possessions possessing you so you can truly follow me." The direction of the denial was to benefit this man spiritually, not destroy him physically and emotionally.

Now, it's at this point most of us ordinary Jesus girls start thinking of all the rich people we know. "Well, I sure hope they get this message. Good thing I'm not rich. Good thing this doesn't apply to me. Good thing Jesus doesn't ask me to sacrifice in this way."

Or does He?

As you can see, I don't think Jesus meant this as a sweeping command for all those who have a lot of money. I think Jesus meant this for any of us who wallow in whatever abundance we have. I think Jesus looked straight into this young man's soul and said, "I want you to give up that which you crave more than me. Then come, follow me."

Piercing thought, right?

Suddenly, Jesus isn't staring at the rich young man, He's staring at me. The inside me. The part I can't cover up with excuses and makeup.

For when Jesus ends His statement with "follow me," it's not an invitation to drag our divided heart alongside us as we attempt to follow hard after God. When Jesus wants us to follow Him — really follow Him — it's serious business.

Mark 8:34 tell us, "If anyone would come after me, he must deny himself and take up his cross and follow me."

With Jesus, if we want to gain, we must give up.

If we want to be filled, we must deny ourselves.

If we want to conquer our cravings, we'll have to redirect them toward God.

If we want to truly get close to God, we'll have to distance ourselves from other things.

Is this really possible? Jesus says with God, it is: "With man this is impossible, but with God all things are possible." Hold on to that, friend. Tuck it in your heart and keep on reading.

We were made to crave. We were made to desire, want greatly, and arrange our life around the filler of our void. We were. But the object of that craving was and is and only should be God. And God alone.

He is the only true filler of our voids.

When we try and fill those voids with other people or things, we'll feel increasingly distant from God.

If we understand how God can fill us, we'll grow closer and closer to Him.

And nothing will get your heart into a more wonderfully fulfilling place than being close to God.

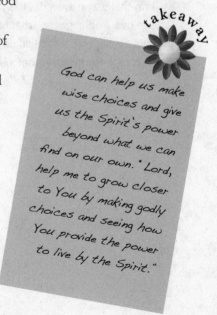

takeaway

God can help us make wise choices and give us the Spirit's power beyond what we can find on our own. "Lord, help me to grow closer to You by making godly choices and seeing how You provide the power to live by the Spirit."

the action plan

Copy this prayer into your journal, and also put it one other place where you will see it this week (your bathroom mirror, your computer monitor, your car dashboard, or the inside of your locker):

"God, I need wisdom to make wise choices. I need insight to remember the words I've read in Scripture. I need power beyond what I can find on my own. Help me to grow closer to You by making godly choices and seeing how You provide the power to live by the Spirit."

Pray that prayer every day this week, and keep an eye out to see how God answers. What happens in your heart *and* in your outward life that could be God answering that prayer? Record those things in your journal.

chapter 9

Tattooed On My Heart

Several years ago I (Lysa) sat beside my youngest sister, who was nineteen at the time, and listened as she boldly rejected my views of God. She's always been a free spirit, much too nonconventional for traditional religion.

"Good thing I'm not into religion," I gently replied.

She twisted her face as if half expecting a lightning bolt to strike us both. "But you *are* religious."

I laid my head against the back of the lounge chair, closed my eyes to the sun now washing over me, and simply replied, "Nope."

Deciding to let my statement just sit for a while, I opted not to clarify unless she asked. And ask she did.

That's when I explained that I follow God, not a religious activity. I want to become more and more like Jesus, not more and more a follower of a religious system of rules. I am passionate about getting into the Bible — God's teachings — and letting the Bible get into me. I no longer evaluate life based on my feelings. Instead, I let my feelings and experiences be evaluated in light of God's Word.

I have watched God chase me around with rich evidence of His presence and invitations to trade apathy for active faith. But I had to make the choice to see God. Hear God. Know God. And follow hard after God.

That day I took my sister's hand and told her I'd be praying for God to mess with her in ways too bold for her to deny.

And mess with her He did.

Fast forward to five years later. My sister walked into a professor's office and saw one of my books on her bookshelf. I don't think my sister really believed anyone actually read my books, but there it was. And it messed with her.

She later went home and poked around my blog a bit, where she found a clip of my testimony. Again, it messed with her. One verse in particular messed with her so much that she let the possibility of God's existence slip into her heart.

A few days later, out of the blue, she went and had *Jeremiah 29:11* tattooed on the back of her neck. That is the wonderful verse that says, " 'For I know the plans I have for you,' declares the LORD, 'plans to prosper you and not to harm you, plans to give you hope and a future.' " She called, wanting to talk to me. About life. About tattoos. And about God.

Then a few weeks later she called again, and I stood in the middle of a busy airport praying for this precious girl who had called asking for those prayers. She had called. She had called again. She had asked. And that's the miracle of our Jesus: He is the God of the impossible.

I wonder what might happen if we dared to ask God for the impossible just a little more often. I'm up for it. Are you?

Filled with the Truth

Which of the three things we've talked about — emotional, physical, and material cravings — seems the most impossible for you to distance yourself from? Because right there is where Satan wants to get in and whisper for you to lay this book aside: *It's too hard. It's not that important. It won't last. It won't make a difference.*

I've heard those lies too. But what if I'd given up on my sister? Don't stop trying. And please understand that I'm not saying we should have a Scripture tattooed on the back of our neck to keep us motivated. Our mother almost had a heart attack when she found out what my sister had done. My thought was, *"Well, it's better than a lot of other things she could have had tattooed!"* But that's beside the point. The point is, we should have truth tattooed on our heart, mentally and spiritually marking our heart with truth in a permanent way.

One key to having God's truth branded on our heart is to know the Bible as well as we can. The more we're full of Scriptures, the greater the chance we'll have of deflecting Satan's lies. Every decision we make should pass through the filter of truth first.

Every decision.

But this won't be the case if we don't have truth inside of us.

Remember earlier in the book, when we talked about the three ways Eve was tempted being the same three ways Jesus was tempted in the desert? What did Jesus do each time He was tempted? He said, "It is written …" and He quoted Scripture. The final Scripture He quoted was from Deuteronomy 6:13, and Jesus directed it right at Satan: "Away from me, Satan! For it is written: 'Worship the LORD your God, and serve him only.'"[1]

And you know what happened? "Then the devil left him, and angels came and attended [Jesus]" (Matthew 4:11).

If there is one crucial, crucial activity that lingers long after you close this book, let it be this one. Memorize God's Word. It's your greatest weapon to make the devil leave. This book is filled with verses to get you started. For now, memorize this one:

Isaiah 49:16: "See, I have engraved you on the palms of my hands ..."

In other words, even when you feel forgotten by everyone else, you are remembered by God. You are loved by God. And while His truths are marking your heart in a permanent way, your name has already marked Him in the most lasting of ways. Even more than a tattoo, you are engraved on the palms of His hands.

An Amazing Thought

It is astounding when you ponder what God is saying in that verse. Think about it this way: Have you ever written something on your hand to jog your memory? Like maybe the pages you have to study for Wednesday's algebra test, or that you're supposed to bring a snack to youth group?

I (Shaunti) must confess that I jot little notes on my hand all the time. So not long ago, I was very affected by something I heard as a pastor and his wife drove me through a poor area of downtown Richmond, Virginia. Old cars littered the streets, warehouses with all their windows broken out were slashed by obscene graffiti, unemployed men and women sat around lifelessly, and it seemed like the very air was heavy with a lack of hope.

As we drove through, the pastor began to tell me stories of his ministry in this area, working with the poor and those with mental illness, the truly downtrodden. One day, after he had preached a short sermon in a park about God's great love, a woman named Mae came up to him with drug-deadened eyes that couldn't hide her anguish. From Mae's story, it was clear she had been looking for love her whole life and had never found it. She was abandoned by her father, had lived in poverty her whole life, had been surrounded by drugs and alcohol from the earliest age, dropped out of school when she had several different children by different fathers, and was now probably in her thirties with no life or hope. She told the pastor, "I just don't know how God can love me." She felt small, lost in a sea of poverty and despair. How could God ever see her, know her, love her?

The pastor noticed that she had written many notes to herself on the palm of her left hand. He asked, "Why do you do that?"

"So I can remember things. I have such a hard time remembering things."

"Does that help?"

"Yes. If I have it on a piece of paper, I'll probably forget to look at it. But with the really important things, when it's written there, it's right in front of me so I see it and remember. I can't lose it or forget it."

The pastor looked at her with compassion. "Sister, that is what God says about you. In the Bible, God says, 'I have written your name on the palms of my hands.' Mae, that means He's written *your name* on His hands. *You* are the really important thing to Him." He took her hand and pointed to line after line of notes on her palm. "Just like these notes are right in front of you, God has your name always in front of Him. He is *always* thinking about you.

Mae, an image of you is always in His mind. He loves you that much."

The woman burst into tears, great sobs as she finally grasped the concept of how much God adored her. Not because she had done anything good, and in spite of everything she had done wrong, *God had written her name on His hand.*

God has me always on His mind. He needs to be always on mine.

We can grasp that concept too. What an amazing, glorious, *freeing* thing to realize that God doesn't just have a surface tattoo: He has us literally engraved on His hand.

the action plan

Memorize Isaiah 49:16: "See, I have engraved you on the palms of my hands." Then take an index card, a piece of paper, or your journal, and draw a simple picture of God's hands, palms up, outstretched to the world. On one of the palms, write your name and a description that you know, in God's truth, applies to you even though you may not always feel like it. For example: "Emily — daughter of the King" or "Keisha — beloved of God."

Keep that card where you can see it, and whenever you look at it, thank God for His great love and ask Him to help you understand this truth.

chapter 10

The Empty Place

At this point in the book, some of you may have no trouble accepting the truth of God's astounding love for us, and feel very comfortable with the idea of going to God in our cravings—even if that isn't always easy. But others ... well, others may feel a bit like the Richmond woman we mentioned at the end of the last chapter: You've had unusually intense brokenness and pain in your background. Your cravings almost overwhelm you, because you are seeking to fill such a profound hole. If so, you may think this is all a bit simplistic, that we can't possibly understand, and that you have so much "stuff" in your past (and present) that you will never feel truly whole and satisfied with God alone.

But we do understand, and God's promises apply to you too. He can fill the cravings of even the deepest lack. I (Lysa) know that from very personal experience.

Longing for a Father

As I trace my fingers back across the timeline of my life, I see many times when spiritual and emotional emptiness left me vulnerable. The shape of my lack was the absence of a biological father. It was as if someone held up my family photo and excised his form from our lives with laser-like precision.

There we were — my mom, my sister, and me — with this misshapen family and a hole that extended way deeper than a destroyed picture. All of him was gone. His face that should have looked upon his children with adoration. His arms that should have worked to provide for us. His feet that I should have been allowed to stand on while he danced me around the den. His mind that should have shared wisdom about why pet hamsters die and why boys sometimes break girls' hearts. His heart that should have been filled with compassion and desire to shelter us from the storms that scared us so.

He took with him so much more than he ever could have imagined. Those few suitcases and plastic crates didn't just contain boxers, ties, old trophies, and dusty books. Somewhere in between his Old Spice and office files were shattered pieces of a little girl's heart.

At some point, I came to the realization that everyone has hurts from their past. And everyone has the choice to either let those past hurts continue to haunt and damage them or to allow forgiveness to pave the way for them to be more compassionate toward others.

But the reality of my dad's abandonment created some unhealthy habits that continued to linger in my life. Emptiness has a way of demanding to be filled. And when I couldn't figure out how to fill what my heart was lacking, my stomach was more than willing to offer a few suggestions. Food became a comfort I could turn to anytime. As you've seen in earlier chapters, I gave in to all the cravings we've talked about in this book. But my most addictive temptation was food.

Food was easy. It was filling. It was available. It became a pattern. And somehow, each time my heart felt a little empty, my stomach picked up on the cues and suggested I feed it instead.

Much of this emotional emptiness stemmed back to that little girl coming home from school and being told, "Your daddy's gone." That one event was so huge, so draining, that it caused me to fill my mind with only negative memories of my dad. In my mind, he never loved me at all.

And you know what? Maybe he didn't. But parking my mind only on negative thoughts about my dad left such a sadness in my heart. Though I've been touched by Jesus and my soul is filled with God's good perspective and healing truths, there was still this very human part of me that felt so incredibly sad when I thought about what never was with my daddy.

Sometimes I could brush off this sadness. But other times it made me angry. And defensive. And hungry.

I honestly never thought any feeling or memory other than sadness was ever possible when it came to my dad. Then one day God surprised me in the most unusual way. I had been praying for God to "unsettle me" and make me aware of all those places I'd become resigned to thinking were impossible to change. I meant food issues, of course, but God knew there were other needs. And an unexpected, sweet memory of my dad rose up that changed my dark perspective.

A Better Place to Park My Mind

I grew up in Florida, which meant no snow ever. But I remember praying for snow. I prayed for it like a revival preacher at a tent meeting, I tell you. If ever there could be snow in Florida, surely a passionate little girl's prayers could open up those heavenly storehouses where all snowflakes are kept.

One night the temperatures dropped surprisingly low and the weatherman called for a freeze, which was a rare thing in our area. How tragic there was no precipitation. It was the one night that snow might have been possible.

It broke my little snow bunny heart.

But the next morning I awoke to the most amazing sight. There were icicles everywhere. Gleaming, dripping, hanging, light-reflecting, glorious icicles were all over the trees in our backyard.

It was magical.

We were the only house on the block with this grand winter display.

Because I was the only girl whose daddy thought to intentionally put sprinklers out on the one night it froze.

I don't know where this memory had been hiding for too many years, but what a gift. Somewhere in the deep, mysterious, broken places of my dad's heart, there was an inkling of love and care for me.

And while this certainly doesn't solve the complications of being abandoned by my dad, it gives me a healthy thought to dwell on where he's concerned — one of those good thoughts the Bible tells us to think about: "Whatever is true, whatever is noble, whatever is right, whatever is pure, whatever is lovely, whatever is admirable — if anything is excellent or praiseworthy — think about such things" (Philippians 4:8). I like to call this "parking my mind in a better spot."

It's so easy to park our minds in bad spots, to dwell and rehash and wish things were different. But to think on hard things keeps us in hard spots and only serves to deepen our feelings of emotional emptiness. This is where pity parties are held, and we all know pity parties can demand an abundance of things we shouldn't indulge in, especially in the amount the party demands. Or they can demand resolutions not to partake at all. But pity parties are a cruel way to entertain, for they leave behind a deeper emptiness than we started with in the first place.

When I had pity parties, there I would sit with a guilt-ridden mind, a bloated stomach, an empty heart, and a soul full of anger that my dad was continuing to hurt me even all these years later.

But this memory gave me a new place to park my mind.

Filling the Emptiness

What about you? If you have something in your life that is causing great emotional emptiness, here is a first step toward healing: Can you think of one positive thing from that situation? Or maybe, despite the pain, something good that happened that never would have happened otherwise. If you can't think of anything right now, ask God to give you some safe place to park your mind; a place that will help you with this draining issue from your past.

Then try walking through Philippians 4:8 with God's

truths—and the truths He sends you—in mind. (A counselor can help you with this, too.) Here's how I did this with the emptiness I felt about my dad, as I tried to follow the instruction of Philippians 4:8 and "think about" these particular things:

Whatever is true: My dad was broken. Only broken daddies leave their children. This isn't a reflection of me; it's simply a sad reflection of the choices he made. But it's also true that he had to reach past his brokenness that one night to set up the sprinklers for his little girl. And as small as this one act was, it was an act of love. There *was* love in his heart for me, somewhere.

Whatever is noble: I don't have to live as the child of a broken parent the rest of my life. I can live as a daughter of the King of Kings, who not only wants me but has promised to never, ever leave me. As a matter of fact, the Bible promises me, "The Lord is near" (Philippians 4:5). And the Lord was near the night of the sprinklers. Though my dad professed to be an atheist, I'm convinced Jesus broke through his tough exterior that night and was near to him. Even if he didn't receive Jesus, my dad was near enough one night to see how beautiful love can be. I hope Dad remembers.

Whatever is right: Everything right and good in this life has God's touch on it. It makes me smile to think there must have been two sets of fingerprints on that old, rusty yellow sprinkler that night. My biological daddy carried it, set it up, and turned it on. But my heavenly Daddy made sure the sprinkler was positioned just right to form icicles that froze the trees and warmed my heart.

Whatever is pure: God has set eternity in the heart of every human being (Ecclesiastes 3:11). So, even with all the darkness that seemed to surround my dad, some pure light of selflessness broke through and gave evidence of something good working within him. Warmth on a cold night. Purity in the midst of messy sin and broken hearts.

Whatever is lovely: God can take ugly and build lovely from it. After all, He's called the Potter, right? From the dust of the earth, He formed human beings. That is a lovely quality about God. That loveliness spilled over and helped my dad think of icicles. Really lovely icicles. And in the midst of a backyard that never saw games of catch, a tree house, or father-daughter talks, there was once a glorious display of lovely that only we had.

Whatever is admirable, excellent, or praiseworthy: I wouldn't say my dad was admirable, excellent, or praiseworthy. But then again, maybe I should. Maybe, like the icicles, there are other memories long forgotten and covered over by the darkness of his cruel departure. In the end, my Lord has taken those shattered pieces of my heart and removed them from the boxes my dad carried away that awful day.

Piece by piece, God has created a mosaic in my heart— one of restoration, healing, and compassion. I am the person I am today in part because of the hurt of being left behind by my dad. I wouldn't have chosen that piece of my mosaic, but how good of God to redeem it.

We must identify our places of emotional emptiness and admit how futile it is to try to fill those places with other things. I realize what I've written here is but a first step in this process. Often these issues are big and complicated and a bit like peeling back the layers of an onion. Just when you think you've tackled a piece of it, you realize there are many layers yet to go.

But for today, finding a gentle memory in the midst of a mess is an excellent start. One that is lovely, and true, and worth looking for.

Hope Instead of Defeat

Wherever you are today, I pray these words encourage you. Maybe you have a story about your dad that is similar to mine. Or maybe your empty place is something totally different, but no less intense.

Perhaps it isn't even something you think should be considered a "major" issue — but it really matters to you. Maybe it was a close friend who has abandoned you, a boy that truly broke your heart, a lack of finances, or another kind of deficiency that makes you feel desperate.

Here's the common thread: desperation can breed defeat. In other words, when what is lacking in life goes from being an annoying feeling to a more desperate ache, we run the risk of compromising in ways we never thought we would.

I find it interesting that a commonly quoted verse about how the devil prowls about like a roaring lion looking for someone to devour is tucked right after the verse that says, "Cast all your anxiety on him because he cares for you. Be self-controlled and alert" (1 Peter 5:7–8).

You see, if we get wrapped up in anxiety about what is lacking in our life — even the very legitimate hurts and problems — and forget to be self-controlled and alert, we are prime targets for Satan to usher us right away from God. We start doubting God, doubting His ability to provide, and justifying our way right into sinful patterns. We lower our standards in ways we never thought we would. That's the kind of defeat I'm talking about.

Yes, desperation breeds defeat:

- A person who thinks she would never steal gets into a financial bind and begins to make small compromising choices, feels more and more desperate, and suddenly finds herself skimming money from the register at work.

- A person who thinks she'd never have sex before marriage feels physically pressured by someone she desperately wants love from, and soon finds herself having a hard time saying no to him.

- A person committed to eating healthy forgets to pack her healthy snacks several days in a row and decides to just zip by the vending machine to grab some chips and a candy bar just this one time — or to not eat at all. And then finds that "one time" becomes "more times" all too easily.

Know that these are devised schemes to lure you away from your commitments. There's a great example of how desperation breeds defeat in the story of Esau from the Old Testament in the Bible. Esau was the older of two twins. He was a skillful hunter while his twin, Jacob, was more of a homebody. The Scriptures say:

Once when Jacob was cooking some stew, Esau came in from the open country, famished. He said to Jacob, "Quick, let me have some of that red stew! I'm famished!" (That is why he was also called Edom.)

Jacob replied, "First sell me your birthright."

"Look, I am about to die," Esau said. "What good is the birthright to me?"

But Jacob said, "Swear to me first." So he swore an oath to him, selling his birthright to Jacob.

Then Jacob gave Esau some bread and some lentil stew. He ate and drank, and then got up and left.

So Esau despised his birthright.

Genesis 25:29–34

The thing that strikes me about this story is how much Esau gave up for just a few moments of physical satisfaction. In this time, the oldest son stood to inherit the bulk of his father's lands, livestock, and wealth—all of which Esau signed away when he sold his birthright. He sacrificed what was good in the long term for what felt good in the short term. He gave up his very identity in a moment of desperation.

But if desperation breeds defeat, victory springs from having hope—getting a vision of how different things could be down the road. Had a true friend of Esau's heard this interaction with Jacob, surely he would have spoken some rationality into Esau's irrational impulses by reminding him of all he had to look forward to as the firstborn son if he would just be patient for a little while longer.

If you are feeling desperation, you need hope. Seek it out. Let the Lord be the "lifter of your head"—and remember that He often works through the godly people in our lives. So find a friend who can encourage you and speak rationality into your irrational impulses. A friend who won't give into the same desperation and negativity, but one who will help you look for the positives, hold you accountable, speak the truth in love, and pray for you. If you don't have a friend who can speak hopeful truths into your heart right now, let me be a voice of reason and encouragement today.

Remember who you are. Remember whose you are. And refuse the compromises.

Fill those empty, desperate places with the truths we've discussed in this chapter and throughout this book. Surround yourself with friends who know biblical truth and who will lovingly speak that into your life. Remember that God promises He has a plan and a future for us—and it is good. Because He loves and treasures you—you are His beloved daughter!

Up to this point in the book, we have laid bare all our secret cravings, and how important it is to satisfy those with God. We know how God sees us and how deeply we are loved. And now we come to the point when we must recognize that regardless of our background or history, and regardless of whether it is easy or hard to see ourselves as God's beloved daughters ... we do have to start acting like it. That will be the subject of Part Four.

takeaway

Desperation breeds defeat. Victory springs from having hope.

the action plan

Think about your birthright as a child of God. What does this mean to you personally? For Esau, it meant he would have been given the honor, blessing, and inheritance as the eldest son. But he traded who he was for what he wanted in the heat of the moment.

Have you ever traded who you are in the heat of the moment? Have you ever just gone with the flow in a conversation with friends and thrown out a cuss word because everyone else was doing it? It might seem small in that moment, but it's denying who you are. And that's not so small.

Write a commitment to guard your identity as a child of God on the inside front cover of your Bible. Each time you come across verses that remind you of your position as a loved child of God, add to what you've already written.

PART FOUR

Walking the Talk

chapter 11

Yell "Charge!" and Take Action

When I was in school, I (Lysa) enjoyed learning about history. I was always fascinated with those scenarios where the course of a life, a war, or a nation could have gone a completely different direction if such-and-such a thing had happened in a different way. The most common examples usually centered on military decisions and actions in wartime—or rather, the *lack* of action.

For example, various military commanders of British troops in the Revolutionary War, and those on both sides in the Civil War, seemed to spend a lot of time planning, strategizing, stockpiling—and never moving out. In a few cases the tide of war could have flowed in a very different direction if a leader had yelled "Charge!" instead of hanging back. How weird would it be to live in the American States of Great Britain, or *not* live in the *United* States of America?

In any great hope, in the achievement of any goal, there comes a point where you have to yell "Charge!" and actually move forward.

And if we truly desire to become satisfied with God alone—instead of with the attention of guys, the pleasure of the hidden food habits, the magnetic pull of a shopping spree, or whatever you struggle with — there comes a point when we have to take action.

No More Excuses

Now, I have to be honest: I used to be the queen of *not* taking action where I knew I needed to. Oh, I was a go-getter in every other area of life, but when it came to addressing my physical cravings, I was like Union general George McClellan, of whom President Lincoln famously said, "He has got the slows."

There were many years where I allowed extra pounds to creep onto my body. And, oh, would I make excuses and justifications instead of taking action. Most women gain some weight when they have kids, and I'd birthed three children, right? I even seemed to gain weight with the two we adopted. I justified this by saying I couldn't help it that I had an unforgiving body type and slow metabolism. I was busy with my kids and my husband and my ministry, and I *deserved* those chocolate chip cookies at the end of an exhausting day.

But in the quiet of my heart, I wasn't settled. The reality was I didn't feel good physically or emotionally. I was plagued by negative thoughts about how I looked. I would catch myself standing in front of the bathroom mirror in tears many mornings, lamenting over which pants could best hide my bulge. I cried out to God and admitted it was crazy to get emotional about my pants, for heaven's sake. The tide of justifications would roll back in, only this time with a spiritual twist: *The world has sold women and girls a bill of goods that to be good we have to be skinny. I am above such worldly things. I'm too concerned with my spiritual growth to be distracted by petty issues such as weight and exercise. God loves me just the way I am.*

While the spiritual justifications sounded good, in my heart I knew better. I knew my weight issue didn't have anything to do with me being above worldly things. If I was honest with myself, my issue was plain and simple: a lack of self-control. I could sugarcoat it and justify it all day long, but the truth was I didn't have a weight problem, I had a spiritual problem. I depended on food for comfort more than I depended on God. And I was simply too lazy to resist the pull of unhealthy food. I was too lazy to make time to exercise.

Ouch. That truth hurt.

The reality is God does love me exactly where I'm at; however, He loves me too much to leave me stuck in a place of defeat. If I am defeated by something, God wants to completely transform that and take me to something better. And once I realized my problem was primarily a lack of self-control, I knew I had to change. I had to force myself to yell "Charge!" and actually *do* something about it.

Getting Motivated

Have you ever been there? My friend Kennedy has. She desperately wanted to fit in with her peers and feel special, but she wasn't into some things that other girls were. She didn't care about the latest fashions, had no interest in hairstyles and makeup, and loathed talking about these things. She also didn't care much for studying. She cared about art — the one thing she felt good at. In a situation that involved drawing, painting, or photography, Kennedy came to life. In the middle of an English or math class, she found herself daydreaming.

Already feeling like she didn't fit in, when everyone else got excited about college, she shut down and checked out. Kennedy pulled back from her friends, stopped paying attention in class, didn't complete her assignments, and ignored her parents' threats, punishments, and warnings about her slipping grades.

That's when her parents made a brilliant move — they gave Kennedy a vision for her future. They loaded her into the family car, bad attitude and all, and headed out of town to tour three amazing art schools. Art schools that required pre-requisite classes like English and math. Art schools that wouldn't consider students without a good grade point average.

The minute Kennedy stepped foot into the first classroom on the tour at the first art school, her bad attitude started to fade, and a smile spread across her face. This is what she wanted.

Suddenly Kennedy had a burning desire to go to art school — but realized she would never get in with her failing grades. So she started studying hard, working hard, and getting great grades. Kennedy was taking healthy action instead of falling back on the unhealthy response she had previously had to her cravings to feel special — which was checking out and shutting down when things didn't go well.

I love that Kennedy's parents gave her a vision beyond her present circumstances — and that the vision helped her step out and take action. That's what we hope we've given you through this book: a vision for more … with God, with your future, and with the choices you are making right now.

Do you see how different things can be when you finally stop waffling and decide to just do? That was what finally happened to me after years of telling myself that "it's what's on the inside that counts" — and ignoring the fact that what was on my inside was clearly a lack of self-control, and an ungodly approach to my cravings. One morning, I simply decided to start exercising, so I went for a run. It made me want to cry, but I kept going, because I knew I needed to take better care of myself.

I soon found that nothing about running was fun until after I finished. But the feeling of accomplishment I felt afterward was fantastic! So each day I would fight through the tears and excuses and make the effort to run. Every day I asked God to give me the strength to stick with it this time. I'd tried so many other times and failed after only a few weeks. But then I found something amazing happening: The more I made my action (running) about spiritual growth and discipline, the less I focused on the weight. For me, since the pounds gained were a signal of satisfying my cravings outside of God, each pound lost was not about getting skinny but evidence of obedience to Him.

And because I had no desire to exercise, I *had* to pray and rely on God. The more I focused on running toward God, the less I thought about my desire to stop. And this verse from the Psalms came to life: "My flesh and my heart may fail, but God is the strength of my heart and my portion forever" (73:26). I realized that as I *actually took action*, God's strength came and replaced my excuses, step by step. Without my action, He would have had nothing to work with, but once I made the first step in obedience, He could prove that His strength really was made perfect in my weakness.

God's Power for Your Life

Kennedy's story, and my story, and the story of every other Jesus girl who has seen God's strength in action, is not about studying, or running, or forcing yourself to eat healthy when you want to skip meals, or turning down the advances of the bad boy who makes you feel so special. It is about realizing God's power to take over your complete weakness as you move forward in the action you *know* He is calling you to take.

And what you discover will be far more profound than simply accomplishing something in the physical realm. After I saw God's miraculous power holding me up one day when I desperately wanted to quit, I found this in my Bible: "Teach me your way, O LORD, and I will walk in your truth; give me an undivided heart, that I may fear your name. I will praise you, O LORD my God, with all my heart; I will glorify your name forever" (Psalm 86:11 – 12).

An undivided heart. That's what my whole journey in conquering my physical cravings was about.

And that is what our journey in conquering and redirecting *all* our cravings must be about.

When it comes to my relationships, my body, or my money, I can't live with divided loyalties. I can either be loyal to honoring God with those things, or loyal to my cravings, desires, and many excuses for not doing what I know I should.

And when you honor the Lord with your actions, He can do amazing things in and through you, especially changing things that you worried would never, ever change. Today, my friend Holly and I run four miles together just about every morning. While I can't say I'm always eager to jump out of bed and start running, I'm always glad I'm doing it once I've started. Not to mention how fantastic I feel when we finish. In addition to the benefit of exercising together, we also use that time to pray together, contemplate decisions, and talk about what God is teaching us.

Amazingly, I'm actually thankful now that I have an unforgiving body and slow metabolism that requires me to exercise, because it has meant I've had to give careful thought to my ways. And now I've purposefully determined that taking action to care for my body—which God calls His temple!—is a top priority. I schedule it. I'm held accountable to each day's appointment because I know Holly will be calling me if I don't show up.

But on a much more important level, stepping out and taking action in this way is a spiritual act of worship. This one act undivides my heart and reminds me of the deeper purposes for doing it. I've learned to embrace the benefits instead of resisting the hardship.

What is it that you need to embrace? Where do you *know*, down deep, that the Lord has been pressing you to step out and take action? Where do you need to stop planning, strategizing, and stockpiling, and instead take a deep breath and yell "Charge!" in order to satisfy your cravings with God alone?

Charging forward can be scary, of course. Temptations to stop, shrink back, excuse, and delay will be everywhere. So real action will require self-control, and it will require ongoing self-discipline—both are prerequisites we'll cover in the next two chapters. But the benefit will be the beauty of an undivided heart that is yielded, every day, to Him.

takeaway

If anything is going to change, you have to stop stalling and take action.

the action plan

By now, you have an idea of the primary areas where action is needed to undivide your heart and release you from the hold of unhealthy cravings. Maybe you need to stand up to a certain crowd of "mean girls" who want you to join in while they ridicule other people, and take the risk that doing so could mean losing their approval. Maybe you need to stop weighing yourself every day before school and defining your whole self-worth by a number on a scale. Whatever it is, it's time to do something about it.

Step One: In your journal, set aside a page or two that you will use for the chapters ahead. Write down your cravings, and specifically the areas where you *will* take action even if you don't know exactly *how* you will do it. This is a promise to yourself and to God.

Step Two: After writing down each craving you need to address, create a system of accountability. Enlist a friend who can be your accountability partner going forward — someone who, once you figure out some specific actions, will know exactly what you have pledged to do, and will ask you whether you have done it. Hopefully, you already are going through this journey with a friend, and can use each other as accountability partners. But if not, enlist a trusted female friend, a parent, or a youth pastor to be an accountability partner. Once you have a game plan (taken from the chapters ahead), ask them to check in every week to see how you are doing — it's amazing how much motivation that will bring!

chapter  12

I'll Have Some Water, Manna, and Self-Control, Please

When my (Shaunti's) little boy was having trouble with self-control in first and second grade, I was tempted to pass it off as "just being a boy." That lasted only until a good friend, who is a pediatric therapist, took me aside, looked me in the eye, and said, "Your son's ability to learn self-control will affect everything else in his life, for the rest of his life. If he has a clinical issue and needs a little extra help to learn self-control [which it turns out he did], you have to get him that intervention. You can't let this go."

She was right, of course. I couldn't.

And you can't let things slide on the self-control front either.

What is it that is so very vital about self-control, and what does it have to do with looking to God to fill our emotional, physical, and material cravings?

Self-control is the ability to control what you say and do—even what you think and feel!—for some greater reason, regardless of how you feel at the moment. So for our purposes, self-control means exercising the strength to overcome temptation. This includes the temptation to give in to the *wrong* way of filling your cravings so you can fill them the right way.

This is by no means easy when you start. As the Greek philosopher Aristotle wrote, "I count him braver who overcomes his desires than him who conquers his enemies; for the hardest victory is over self."

But exercising self-control is just like exercising any muscle: it may be hard at first, but it gets much easier, much more quickly than you might think. Your self-control in an area of craving may well be weak at first, but the more you use it (especially when it is difficult) the stronger your self-control will be when you most need it.

Self-Indulgence versus Self-Control

The problem, of course, is that by definition you need self-control the most when you don't want to use it! I had to laugh when I ran across this comment from an old columnist named Franklin P. Jones: "What makes resisting temptation difficult for many people is they don't want to discourage it completely."

The three cravings, after all, just *beg* for us to indulge them. Honestly, they are often the Three Compulsions, not just the three cravings!

You feel *compelled* to check your text messages in the morning the moment you get out of bed, and one hundred other times during the day.

You feel *compelled* to call your boyfriend and ask why he hasn't texted you back.

You feel *compelled* to buy that new lip gloss or eye shadow, even though you already have eleven similar shades in your makeup drawer.

You feel *compelled* to try on those outfits at the mall after a bad day at school, even though you know you really can't afford them.

You feel *compelled* to grab a bowl of ice cream to eat while you're watching the late-night movie on television — even though you're not hungry and, truth be told, already had too much sugar today.

You feel *compelled* to go for a run to burn off the calories you ate, even though you barely ate anything.

Whatever your compulsion is, whatever craving it represents, there comes a point when you have to choose between self-control and self-indulgence. And that choice will make the difference between whether you master the temptation or it masters you.

The world isn't going to help you with this, by the way. "The whole world is under the control of the evil one," the apostle John warns us (1 John 5:19), which means the world is the source of those temptations, not the solution.

And this means that there will *always* be those triggers that come on hard days:

> The group was talking about me behind my back, and I feel completely rejected. I want an Oreo. Or ten.
>
> I hate cleaning my room; I'll never be organized like Lara. When I'm done I'll treat myself by downloading all those songs I've wanted.
>
> I completely bombed that important test. I feel so stupid. Maybe if I just *happen* to ride past Jack's house when he gets home, he'll see me and stop to talk.
>
> I don't feel pretty. I need a new hairstyle ... or a new diet plan.

My parents are driving me crazy. I feel like I can never be good enough for them. Those cute new shoes will make me feel a lot better.

It's my birthday, and I don't think anyone really cares. I'll call Justin and see if he wants to see me.

Yes, in a fallen world, there will always be triggers: days when part of you says, "I've been so careful about my cravings, but today is a day I deserve a break. Or a treat. Just one day of doing whatever I want." But "just one" is an open door, because it is all too easy to drop our guard and fall back into old habits. It's such a slippery slope.

I'm not saying we shouldn't allow ourselves the occasional treat. We should. I'm not saying that God won't use earthly things like the listening ear of a friend for comfort. He probably will.

But I've realized when the desire for comfort of any kind is triggered by difficult emotions, it's not really a desire for a break, treats, or healthy comfort — it's a thinly veiled attempt at self-medication. And *that* is when we most need to practice self-control, since any attempt to self-medicate with a shopping spree, hunger, food, sex, or the approval of friends can trigger a vicious cycle we must avoid.

It's also important to note that not all of our indulgence is caused by emotional responses. Let's just be honest, shall we? Sometimes we simply lack the self-control to say enough is enough.

A Lesson in Self-Control ... Through Portion Control

A few years ago, as I (Lysa) was struggling with my physical cravings, the words *portion control* took on new meaning as I studied a familiar story in the book of Exodus. I noticed the curious emotional response God's people had after Moses led them out of slavery in Egypt. God's people had just seen Him do giant miracle after giant miracle to free every one of them from Egypt and help them escape their captors, but for some reason they panicked when it came to trusting God to meet their needs in the much more mundane area of food to eat. So this really must have been their "issue" — a craving that they secretly looked to for security, instead of God. In the desert the whole community grumbled against Moses and Aaron. The Israelites said to them, "If only we had died by the LORD's hand in Egypt! There we sat around pots of meat and ate all the food we wanted, but you have brought us out into this desert to starve this entire assembly to death."

> Then the LORD said to Moses, "I will rain down bread from heaven for you. The people are to go out each day and gather enough for that day. In this way I will test them and see whether they will follow my instructions."
>
> Exodus 16:2–4

In other words, God was going to use the one thing the Israelites most looked to for comfort and security to teach them daily dependence on Him. Don't you love how applicable this is to us?

It gets even better. Look at that last line: *"I will test them and see whether they will follow my instructions."* As the rest of the story makes clear, God was also teaching them obedience and self-control as *the way* in which they would conquer their cravings, fears, and worries, and come to that true dependence on Him. In every area of our lives, I don't think we can learn dependence without self-control.

So here's how He taught His ancient people to exercise self-control. Interestingly, it wasn't by asking them to completely give up what they craved. Don't ever believe the lie that God secretly wants to deny you everything you enjoy. God desires good things for His children. Instead, God taught His people self-control by asking them to view this amazing bounty laid out before them — — *and to obey His instructions about taking only a certain amount of it!*

As the story continues, each day the Israelites depended on God for their portion of food. Then God would rain down exactly what they needed for nourishment. It was called *manna*, which I imagine was something like little sweet potato flakes. God instructed the Israelites to go out each morning and collect only enough manna that each needed for that one day. He also instructed them to *not* try to save some of it for the next day.

Trusting God to bring them miracle food in the desert wasn't just an exercise in dependence; this portion restriction was a lesson in self-control. Imagine that you were wandering in that desert and there was no food anywhere — certainly not enough animals or plants to feed hundreds of thousands of people. So when the ground was covered in manna in the morning, how tempting it would be to ignore God's command, indulge your fears, and gather up as much as you could? *Just in case God doesn't come through tomorrow, I'll at least have a few days of food stored up.* Or even if you obeyed on the portion amount, it would be tempting to try to save at least some of it. Just in case.

But God needs His people to learn self-control. So when

some people inevitably tried to store some of the manna, they found that it was stinky and slimy with maggots the next morning. Blech! That was one way for God to not let people get away with overindulgence or disobedience!

Interestingly, God's only exception to the one-day-portion rule was the day before the Sabbath, a day God had set aside for the people to rest and not do work — like gathering food. He told the people to gather a double portion the day before, so they wouldn't have to work on the holy day. And guess what? On that day alone, the stored manna was fresh and good to eat instead of rotten.

God didn't want to deprive His people, but He didn't want the spiritual decay that came with overindulging their cravings, either. The Israelites were never to gather up extra and build big storehouses of manna supplies where they could set up drive-thru windows for McManna Happy Meals. No, this was God-given portion control as His way to teach self-control. And of course the whole process would put them in the habit of depending on God, and only God, every single day.

In our day, we would do well to apply this same process to our struggles, whatever they are. Each day God will be the perfect portion of everything we need — every longing we have, every desperate desire our souls cry out for. With this in mind, let's revisit a few of the emotional struggles we noted earlier that often trigger a desire to indulge our cravings.

My friends are talking about me behind my back. Instead of grabbing the tube of Oreos or signing up for the latest diet plan, I ask God to be my daily portion of companionship in this lonely time. "God, I hate this rejection and hurt. Sometimes I feel like the loneliness is going to swallow me alive. I can't deal with this on my own. Will You be my portion of healing and companionship for this day?"

I completely bombed that important test. Instead of riding past Jack's house six times in the hope that he'll just "happen" to see me, stop to talk, and leave me feeling better about myself, I ask God to be my portion of strength as I sit for a few minutes and write this in my prayer journal instead: "God, I so desperately want comfort right now and seeing Jack seems like it would be so comforting. It hurts so much that I am going to get a grade I can't afford to get. Feeling like a failure makes me want to say 'Who cares' and do whatever will make me feel better. Will You be my portion of comfort and strength and success in this moment?"

My parents are driving me crazy, so I said something sarcastic, blasted out of the house in irritation, and drove to the mall. Instead of laying out my summer-vacation cash for that cute (and expensive) pair of shoes that catches my eye, I pray, "God, I don't want to be a disrespectful daughter. I feel so misunderstood, and when I feel like this I don't know if I have it in me to always be patient and respectful the way the Bible asks. But I know my parents love me, even when I don't feel like it's true. And with Your portion of strength I can rely on You in this moment—instead of medicating my jangling feelings at the shopping mall—and go make it right with my parents."

Whatever the situation, keep asking God to be your daily portion—of companionship, provision, patience—over and over. And one day you will find victory over those things instead of just looking back over a pile of tears and Oreo crumbs. Here's a biblical promise we can rely on:

> Because of the LORD's great love we are not consumed, for his compassions never fail. They are new every morning; great is your faithfulness. I say to myself, "The LORD is my *portion*; therefore I will wait for him."
>
> Lamentations 3:22–24, emphasis added

Grasping the truth that God is our portion, *and using the self-control to act like it,* has the potential to transform more than just bad habits; it can transform our responses to every aspect of our lives. Practicing self-control to learn God's portion control was crucial for the spiritual development of the Israelites, and it's crucial for our spiritual development as well.

Whether we are talking about guys, friends, food, body image, new clothes, or anything else we abuse to try to fill ourselves, nothing in this world can ever fill us like God's portion. Nothing else can truly satisfy. Nothing else is unfailing and absolute. And we don't say all this with a quirky little smile, hoping it works. We shout it from the depths of our souls because we *know* it works, "for he satisfies the thirsty and fills the hungry with good things" (Psalm 107:9).

takeaway

God has His portion of strength for me in every temptation that I face.

the action plan

Did this chapter remind you of any additional areas of craving in which you need to exercise self-control and fight temptation? If so, write those in your journal.

The next time you're faced with a need for self-control in *any* of the areas you have identified, stop what you are doing for a moment and walk away to pray. Ask God for that portion of strength, that you might have the self-control to do the wise and healthy thing. Journal about what happens.

chapter  13

From Desires to Discipline

I f self-control is primarily about stopping yourself from doing something that your tempted heart is crying out for, self-discipline is about building the ability to do that regularly, and training yourself to do the thing that is much, much better. In other words, *self-discipline* involves systematically building the habits that will make walking away even easier—or that will keep you away from temptation (and thus the need for self-control) in the first place.

Self-control means wrenching yourself away from your boyfriend when you are kissing and things are getting a little too hot and heavy. Self-discipline means never putting yourself in a make-out situation to begin with.

Self-control means not tweeting about the friend who ditched plans to join you for a movie when something else came along she wanted to do. Self-discipline means making an internal commitment to never say dishonoring things about others, because it hurts them and will often come back to haunt you.

Self-control means looking at the bag of M&M's in the pantry and forcing yourself to close the door. Self-discipline means a habit of only allowing yourself chocolate once a week as a dessert, so dipping into the bag as a snack today isn't even an option.

Self-control means not throwing away your lunch even though your friends trash theirs. Self-discipline means getting into a habit of eating three balanced meals per day, and including all foods in moderation.

Self-control means looking at the expensive-but-adorable outfit on the rack and forcing yourself not to try it on. Self-discipline means a habit of checking your bank balance before you go, deciding how much you will spend — and taking only that amount of cash into the mall.

In the last chapter, we talked about self-control being like a muscle that gets much stronger the more you use it. The hard work of self-discipline is the main reason for that growing strength. And the beautiful thing is your hard work creates a self-perpetuating cycle. Being self-disciplined makes the process of self-discipline itself easier and easier!

Self-Discipline 101

When I (Shaunti) was in college, I was in one of the school's big extravaganza musical productions. Now, being in a show wasn't unusual for me; I was heavily involved in musical theater growing up and had been in dozens of shows over the years. To this day, although I can't remember the year the Magna Carta was signed, how a calculus function works, or the capital of Mongolia, I can probably remember the words to every verse of every song of every popular musical to appear on Broadway.

So being in a show wasn't new. What was new was that this was my first *college* show — in an intense, well-regarded program that suffered no fools. The college director and choreographer didn't care that in high school I'd been the lead in this show or the dance captain in that show. *Everyone* had. I had to prove myself at a much higher level.

The other new thing was much more intimidating: this was the tap-dancing musical *Anything Goes*. And I had never once taken a tap lesson. At my audition, the choreographer and director evaluated my general dancing ability and said, "We think you can do it, but you're going to have to learn fast."

The rehearsals for that show became daily five-hour-long boot camp sessions for me—and a lot of the other cast members. We weren't just rehearsing to learn the steps (and in my case to learn tap); we were getting into condition to survive the run of the show without having a heart attack. Each time the curtain went up and we performed the show, we would be enduring a three-hour-long tap-dancing marathon—with smiles on our faces and singing on pitch at the same time. So the dance captains got us in shape as ruthlessly as any drill sergeant, pushing us through hundreds of painful ab crunches, leg lifts, squats, and push-ups each day. We drilled the songs and the sequences for hours at a time. In addition, I had to stay an hour after rehearsal ended at ten o' clock each night to learn tap. And of course, on top of that, I also had these other little duties called economics tests, government papers, and marketing projects . . .

I'll be honest—I had never really needed to be all that self-disciplined before, in any area of my life. Music and dance came fairly naturally to me, as did schoolwork. Sure, I had to show up to rehearsal (although usually late), I had to run my lines, I had to study a bit for tests. But I found that I could do fine without really being *disciplined* about it. I could get away with sitting down with a favorite "beach read" novel and losing hours at a time in the story, or stealing a few hours at the mall with a friend even when I had a paper due the next day. Obviously, there's a place in life for downtime, but I simply didn't know what it meant to truly be a good steward of the gifts God had given me.

But that all had to change. If I wanted to be a part of the show — and not flunk out of school — no one was going to get me there but me. And that meant self-discipline at a level I'd never even glimpsed before. I had to have the discipline to finish the third set of crunches when my abs were screaming for mercy. I had to discipline myself to do the exercises effectively even when the dance captains/slavemasters were out of the room. Even though I am the furthest thing from a morning person, I had to create and stick with a practice of getting up to do at least an hour or two of homework *before* my eight o'clock geology lab every Monday, Wednesday, and Friday morning, since I knew I would have no time for homework after rehearsal and tap lessons. When I had a precious free hour, I had to have the self-control to say no to reading novels that sucked away so much time, and instead discipline myself to work on the research paper that wasn't due for two months.

And here's the amazing part: all of that was hard the first few weeks, easier the next few, and by the second month, I couldn't imagine *not* having this discipline in my life. I noticed that the more disciplined I was about getting up early to study, the more able I was to control my tongue when I wanted to shred someone who had been rude to me. The more I disciplined myself to finish *all* the exercise sets, even when someone wasn't looking, the more disciplined I was about getting up at six in the morning when the alarm blared, instead of hitting snooze. I even started naturally showing up places on time!

When the show ended and my life suddenly returned to "normal," I realized—I didn't want it to. I was *grateful* for the self-discipline that now extended into many different areas of my life. I didn't want to lose the practice of self-discipline in one area that made all other self-discipline easier.

Looking back, I realized something else: the purpose of that time in my life had very little to do with the show. I knew I was never destined to be a Broadway star; I pursued economic analysis and Wall Street, and God eventually led me toward social research, writing, and public speaking. These were all areas where I needed to have a strong work ethic. Where I couldn't procrastinate. Where I had to put down my beach-read novels and meet tough deadlines … In other words, areas that would require me to work hard instead of coasting along.

All of that experience wasn't about the show. It was about God using an area of weakness and laziness in which I needed to be strong, to help me learn the habit and practice of self-discipline; a habit and a practice that would help me overcome *any* area of weakness for the rest of my life, if I chose to let it.

What is your area of need or weakness? Which cravings have a hold on you that you want to change? In which craving-weakness do you need to establish a habit and a practice of self-discipline in order to train up those muscles? Rest assured that God will use those habits of self-discipline in amazing ways that go far beyond what you can imagine right now.

Habits of Self-Discipline

- NOT checking Facebook first thing in the morning, so you get over your addiction.

- NOT walking by the doughnut case at Quik Trip — if you don't see it, you can't buy it.

- NOT counting calories (if you're tempted to eat too little) to figure out if you've been "good" or "bad" today.

- NOT sending multiple texts to the guy you went out with recently, just because you're lonely.

- NOT "keeping your options open" when invited to a friend's house for Friday night, just in case you get a "better offer" and are invited to go to that party you've heard rumors about.

- NOT checking email or surfing the web so often you don't get work done. *(Gee, we can't imagine why that would come up while we're on a book deadline.)*

- TO do a quiet time with God first thing, before your day gets busy.

- TO take one slice of buttered toast, not two. (Or, if you're tempted to eat too little, TO always eat meals, instead of skipping.)

- TO cut up cucumbers or steam some broccoli even if your mom doesn't, so you have some veggies and fiber along with the hamburger.

- TO spend a few minutes writing in your prayer journal when upset by a bad grade instead of first jumping in the car to go shopping.

- TO put things you want to buy on hold instead of just reflexively buying them, and telling the clerk you'll come back in an hour after you've thought about it.

- TO transfer 10 percent of your "shopping money" to the "tithe" section in your cash envelope or bank account as a way of going to God with your material cravings.

Discipline Is Always a Specific Action

As we have been on this journey in this book, I'll bet that you've been hearing some little ringtones from God drawing your attention to areas you don't always like to think about. I'm assuming that in His own distinctive, gentle way, He's been calling to you about a few areas that you need to work on. And working on them will require specific actions that become specific habits. "I need to eat healthier" is not an action. "I will only eat sweets twice a week" or "I will eat a healthy protein, fruit, and vegetable at each meal" is an action that becomes a habit—a permanent discipline you can follow.

There are unlimited possible actions, but to get you started, the sidebar on page 136 has some examples of simple actions that address each of the areas of craving we've been talking about in this book. And when you commit to the actions that address your areas of weakness, as a permanent pattern, it leads to a lifestyle of self-discipline.

So what permanent pattern do you need to establish? In the chart that follows, capture at least two or three of the things *you* know you need to work on, and what action or actions of self-discipline would help you begin to address each one.

For example, suppose you now recognize that with each of your boyfriends you have gone further physically than you should, because you are being driven by a deep emotional craving for a guy's affection. Your area of craving-weakness might be, "I have an emotional craving to feel that someone loves me." One of your areas of discipline might be, "I will resolve to never be alone with a boyfriend in a room with the door closed. I will not put myself in a make-out situation."

Or perhaps you recognize that you eat for comfort, munching on treats when you aren't hungry. You might write, "I have a physical craving to comfort myself with food." Your area of discipline might be, "When I crave a snack but I am not hungry, I will resolve to *not* walk into the kitchen, and will instead pray for a few minutes about what is going on in my life." Or maybe even, "I will seek help from a nutritionist to completely change my eating habits."

Take a moment now to jot down your answers on the chart below.

My craving-weakness	My discipline: what I need to do differently

You may think, "No way are those types of self-discipline possible over the long run." But from personal experience, we can both tell you that they are. You just have to decide. Then, once you have made that decision, there are a few important strategies that will help you stick to your decision over time. Those are the subject of the next chapter.

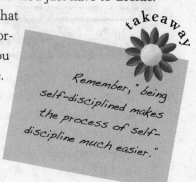

takeaway

Remember, "being self-disciplined makes the process of self-discipline much easier."

the action plan

In your journal, you now have a list of problem areas (from chapters eleven and twelve) in which you need to take action. In the sidebar on page 138, you also outlined some steps of self-discipline you will take in one or more areas. Take a few minutes to apply those same kinds of tactics to the list in your journal. What specific steps of self-discipline will you take? What are the personal guidelines you will set up and stick to?

Remember: these action steps have to be specific and allow you to check whether you are doing them or not. Something like "I'll make better choices with friends" is not a 'checkable' action or rule of self-discipline. Instead, "I will not go to a friend's party unless I'm sure a parent will be there" is a rule of self-discipline. It is clear whether you are doing it or not.

What you will end up with is a list of cravings that you are addressing and a specific action you will take, or rules you will adhere to, that will help you fight temptation and lead you to healthy choices on each.

Finding the Power to Say No

As you now know, one of my (Lysa's) great weaknesses was in the area of going to food instead of to God—especially to comfort foods loaded with sugar and other unhealthy carbs. When I decided I had to change, I realized I would have to do it very differently than I had attempted before. Whatever your area of craving temptation, you may have to do it differently too—because all too often, our best efforts are simply temporary. If you have tried for a while, and been disappointed in the end, it is very likely that your efforts, like mine, were simply based on drumming up willpower and discipline for a season, rather than truly allowing God to transform you.

In my past efforts to confront my physical cravings, lose weight, and get healthy, I had done some serious diets and had shed excess pounds—for a while. By definition, since I was on a "diet," I knew somewhere, deep down, that it was a temporary deprivation, a temporary discipline, and that there would come a day that I wouldn't have to be so strict about what I ate. Mentally, I always had an escape hatch—and since I hadn't dealt with the underlying cravings that were driving me to food, there always came the day when I opened the escape hatch and fled.

I was like an alcoholic who resolved to stay sober—but who felt like he could always handle a glass of wine or two at a party ... or go to a bar every now and again ... or keep that bottle of vodka in the cupboard just in case ...

But as anyone who has been around alcoholics knows, the only way they can overcome their addiction permanently is to come to a point when they decide that they will stay completely sober and never have a drink of alcohol again. And I was just as addicted to the comfort and pleasure of consuming food as an alcoholic is to drinking an intoxicating beverage. So just like an alcoholic, I needed a self-discipline that would not allow an escape hatch, but would eliminate it altogether.

I realized I needed a strict eating plan: a no-sugar, balanced, healthy-carbs-and-protein plan. That doesn't sound so bad until you realize sugar is in just about everything we enjoy eating: breads, pasta, potatoes, and rice, not to mention all things bakery-licious.

I did fine for a while, but there inevitably came a day that I was having a special dinner on a special vacation and started to have a little pity party. I squirmed in my chair and thought, *I'll just take one little bite ... maybe two ... I've been so good ... I even exercised this morning ... This is vacation ... Everyone else is indulging ... This isn't fair ...*

The sugar was like a siren from mythical tales, luring the ships over to rocky coves that would inevitably dash and destroy the vessel. The seduction was smooth and seemingly oh-so innocent—like it hardly mattered. But in that moment of temptation, I realized having a pity party was a clue I was relying on my own strength, a strength that had failed me before and would fail me again. And thinking it didn't really matter was a lie from the enemy to tempt me to lower my guard and start carving out that escape hatch after all.

It's at this exact point when the dieter on vacation indulges, the virgin sleeps with her prom date, the girl on a debt reduction plan pulls her credit card back out for a big sale, the alcoholic skips AA and heads off to her friend's beer-laden birthday bash instead. There will always be a point when we are tempted to rationalize: "Special times deserve special exceptions, and anything else just isn't fair. It's just this once ..."

I realized at that moment that I had to have far more than simply good, daily discipline habits for eating well, and the self-control to not eat that tempting item sitting before me. Instead, I needed a practice and a habit of grabbing hold of God's strength and inviting His power into the situation whenever I was tempted—for the rest of my life. I needed a constant, *permanent* discipline and strategy I could apply each time I started to look for that escape hatch again.

I felt like the answer would be a go-to script I could cling to in those moments. Some thought, some truth that would allow God to come in strength and transform my weakness. But what was it? Struggling with the beautiful dessert at that beautiful dinner on that beautiful vacation, I lowered my head and prayed, "God, I am at the end of my strength here. This is the moment I've got to sense Your strength stepping in. The Bible says Your power is made perfect in weakness. This would be a really good time for that truth to be my reality. Help me see something else besides this temptation looming so large in front of me it seems impossible to escape."

Suddenly a memory flashed across the screen of my mind. I was sitting on my back deck with my teenage son and his girlfriend, having a deeply honest and gut-wrenching conversation. They had gotten into a bad situation and allowed things to go too far physically. While not every boundary line was crossed, they had crossed enough to scare them both. My advice to them was to think beyond the moment. To say out loud, "This feels good now, but how will I feel about this in the morning?"

That was it. I was challenged by the words and expectations I had placed on my son while not realizing how this same advice could be so powerful if applied to my area of struggle. I had my go-to script. As I asked myself, *This feels good now, but how will I feel about this in the morning?* God's power filled in the gap of my weakness.

Soon, it was time to get up from the dinner table. I pushed back my chair, left the dessert untouched, and walked back to our room. And I've never felt so empowered in my life.

Now, of course that action was the response I needed in *my* area of struggle with food. You may have a totally different struggle. Or, you may struggle with food in the opposite direction—by depriving yourself of it. If that's you, then feeling empowered through walking away from food is exactly what you *don't* need. In fact, that feeling of power and control is what you are indulging when you deny your body what it needs—so your go-to script will lead you to a completely different action. A girl named Rachel told us this story:

> I was sixteen years old and spring break was right around the corner—and so was my bathing suit. I felt fat regardless of what size I was, and thought all my friends had better bodies. I dreaded the moment when I would walk out on the beach with my friends,

peel off my cover-up, and reveal my imperfections for the world to judge.

The year before I had tried to stop eating in the months before spring break, and when I would eat I would stick to low-calorie, low-fat stuff. When I would lose control and overeat, I would throw up or exercise an insane amount to make up for it. I shed pounds, but I was woozy all the time, irritable, and distant from my friends and family because I was keeping such a big secret. Plus, when I started eating normal foods again, I gained back all the pounds, plus more — without even overeating! I guess my body had been so desperate for food it hung on to whatever it could get. I felt so discouraged, embarrassed, and miserable.

Lucky for me, shortly after that I met an older girl who'd struggled with anorexia and bulimia and overcome it. She helped me to finally, truly believe that my worth was not based on my weight or appearance. That God made me and He didn't make mistakes. And that all foods were acceptable — the best thing to do was pay attention to my hunger and fullness, signals I'd long since forgotten while obsessing over diet plans. Funny how I didn't overeat or gain weight when I focused on my body's natural cues. I was feeling happy and so free, and my friends and family noticed.

And then February rolled around again. One day, several of my friends threw lunches away to start getting ready for spring break. I didn't know what to do, because I knew where that behavior would take me, but the thought of a bathing suit made it awfully hard to not diet. Then I remembered: *Your worth is not based on your appearance.* God made you and He doesn't make mistakes.

I repeated that to myself, walked past the trash can, sat down, and pulled out the sandwich, the chips, the yogurt, and the dessert. The dessert! Can you believe it? What a victory. I sat there with my friends that day and ate all my food, because that's how much it took to feel comfortably full. Other days my body needed less, but I still ate from all food groups, including sweets. And I repeated my affirmations a lot. *Your worth is not based on your appearance. God made you and He doesn't make mistakes.* Sometimes I'd add other ones like: *I'm going to choose to take care of my body by eating lunch, and it's okay to eat dessert.*

Spring break finally came, and I don't even remember peeling off my cover-up, because I was too busy laughing with my friends, something I couldn't have done a year earlier when I was so preoccupied with food. My body may not be the media's definition of perfect, but with God's help I've chosen to accept it and thank God for how He made me!

Girls, finding the script that speaks to your cravings is so important. For Rachel, it was, "Your worth is not based on your appearance. God made you and He doesn't make mistakes." For me it was "This feels good now, but how will I feel about it later?" Or maybe God empowers you more as you mentally recite the go-to script I mentioned in a previous chapter: "I am made for more. I am made for victory."

Or, if you had to learn a lot of Bible verses in Sunday school, you might want to recall Scriptures that you have banked up in your heart, ones you can use when you face the temptation to indulge, to compromise, to give in: "I'm more than a conqueror." "With God all things are possible." "Let the peace of God reign in your heart." "Lead us not into temptation but deliver us from the evil one ..."

Ask God to show you the discipline that will work for you; the go-to script that will help you rely on His strength and not yours. And use it. Make it a habit, and never stop.

Some time after my turning-point victory on that vacation, I looked up that verse about God's strength being a perfect match for my weakness:

> But [Jesus] said to me, "My grace is sufficient for you, for my power is made perfect in weakness." Therefore I will boast all the more gladly about my weaknesses, so that Christ's power may rest on me. That is why, for Christ's sake, I delight in weaknesses, in insults, in hardships, in persecutions, in difficulties. For when I am weak, then I am strong.
>
> 2 Corinthians 12:9 – 10

God's power is made perfect in weakness. This stirs my heart. Weakness is difficult, but weakness doesn't have to mean defeat. It is my opportunity to experience God's power firsthand. Had I said yes to that one bite that first night of our vacation, there would have been more compromises. Compromise built upon compromise equals failure.

By contrast, seeing God come through allowed promise upon promise to be built up in my heart. That creates such joy — such empowerment! This is God's power working through my weakness. As I left that dining room, I knew one day I would be empowered enough to take a couple of bites and walk away, but that day had not yet come.

Whatever you are struggling with today, Shaunti and I can assure you that God is fair and just. We can assure you that He wants to take your yielded areas of weakness and use them to teach you permanent disciplines and strategies that will bring His goodness and His power into every other area of your life.

takeaway

Ask yourself, "This feels good now, but how will I feel about it in the morning?"

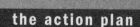

the action plan

Take a moment to pray and ask God to show you which truths you can cling to in your moments of weakness — which go-to scripts would be the most transformative for you. Go back and skim this chapter if you need ideas. In particular, skim the Scriptures we have discussed so far in this book and see if any can be used as scripts for you.

Write all those script options in your journal — any that speak to you. Then pick those that you think will be most helpful and write them on an index card, on a sticky note, or enter them into your phone — somewhere you can refer to them when you need affirmation or help. The next time you are tempted, ask God for His strength and use your go-to script. Journal what happens.

chapter 15

What If I Let God Down?

Recently, I received an email from a friend that said, "Lysa, one of my greatest fears in reading *Made to Crave* is not just letting myself down, but even worse, letting God down."

I understand how she feels. Maybe you're having that same feeling right now. What if you really try this "craving God thing"—you try self-control and self-discipline, you try to rely on God's strength—and you mess up?

What if you feel great for a couple of months, make wise choices, and then you return to old habits?

I understand where you're coming from. When I wrote *Made to Crave* for adult women, I was very honest about my physical struggles with food. A doctor had labeled me obese, which meant this wasn't just an issue of me wanting to be a little thinner—my struggles were now a health issue as well. I had to do something to get healthier.

The problem was I'd tried every diet I knew before and always had the same results. I'd lose the weight, deceive myself into thinking I could return to old habits, and all the weight would creep back on. I'd failed at finding lasting victory with every other attempt, even with programs

I thought were a sure thing. So why would this one be any different?

And why in heavens would I want to add spiritual guilt on top of my physical guilt by turning to God to help me? Why would I risk the shame of making God look bad too?

Maybe you know about physical guilt because you struggle with an eating disorder in the other direction. Have you ever been caught in a binging and purging cycle, or restricted your intake to an extreme? Or maybe your main struggle isn't so much a physical craving as it is an emotional or material one—one in which you've made a commitment to God ... and then blown it.

Suppose you've promised God that you won't text boys late at night, since you know it's just part of a desperate need to feel special—and you went too far physically with your last boyfriend because that need led to wanting more. But suddenly that cute guy texts you ... and you slip. One night of sending texts leads to two, which leads to setting your heart on that dangerous old path. Soon your mind is filled with longings for him more than longings for God. And you fall, again. Instead of turning things around, you feel like you've let God down. Maybe, you think, learning to satisfy life's deepest desires with God isn't possible.

Or perhaps you know God is asking you to forgo spending any money on clothes for three months, since you already have a closet full of stuff you've picked up in a desperate attempt to feel trendy and new. You made a commitment to God that you would give up shopping cold turkey for a time, and you even force yourself to wear the scuffed old shoes to get over your pride in your appearance. But then comes the day you blow it big and drive home with a garment bag full of new clothes and a sinking feeling in your stomach. Maybe, you think, learning to satisfy life's deepest desires with God isn't possible.

Girls, I have news for you: it is. I endured many failed attempts to conquer my cravings during the process of learning how to have victory. Don't believe the lie that this is the way you are made, and you can't find peace. You can.

The Way of Peace

Personally, when I was deep in my struggle, I hated feeling so defeated all the time. It's awful to battle something so raw, so deeply personal, with outward indications apparent to everyone else. The physical struggle was hard enough; I certainly didn't want to drag down my spiritual life with this struggle as well.

But here's the problem: my issues were already dragging me down physically *and* spiritually, whether I admitted it or not. When I don't have peace physically, I don't have peace spiritually. Whatever our temptations are, when we do give in to them we are simply unsettled and lack peace ... which is as it should be, because we need spiritual motivation to step in where our physical determination falls short.

Odds are, we're *all* going to fall short at some point in the journey; changing any habit takes time, and learning to resist the lures of things we once thought were helping us isn't easy. The important thing is that we keep trying, and focus our hearts on the commitment to crave the One that will truly make us happy.

And when you mess up — once, twice, even more — that doesn't mean everything is lost. You've overcome a major hurdle by simply starting the journey in this book, and deciding there is a craving you want to overcome. God understands that, and He can forgive you for any "failure" you may feel: He also wants to help you, be there for you, keep you strong, and show you the person you were made to be.

Remember the statement from an earlier chapter, "I am made for more"? Well, Ephesians 1:17–20 helps unpack that reality even further:

> I keep asking that the God of our Lord Jesus Christ, the glorious Father, may give you the Spirit of wisdom and revelation, so that you may know him better. I pray also that the eyes of your heart may be enlightened in order that you may know the hope to which he has called you, the riches of his glorious inheritance in the saints, and his incomparably great power for us who believe. That power is like the working of his mighty strength, which he exerted in Christ when he raised him from the dead and seated him at his right hand in the heavenly realms.

Now, I realize it's hard to take a verse like this, hold it up to a decadent piece of chocolate cake, and instantly feel a desire to walk away. It's hard to take a verse like this and instantly resist the temptation to skip meals or purge. It's hard to take a verse like this and feel instantly empowered to resist checking how many people liked and commented on what you put on Facebook last night before your read your Bible in the morning. But, if we unpack this verse, understand its richness, and then practice its truth, it's amazing how empowered we'll be even in the face of mistakes. So let's look at some key words and phrases.

Keep Asking

First, "I keep asking." We must ask God to join us in this journey. And this won't be a one-time exercise; Paul (who is credited with writing Ephesians) doesn't ask that this truth be lived out one time for one situation. Paul asks over and over and over again, and so should we. We need to ask for God's wisdom, revelation, and intervening power to be an integral part of our choices from now on.

Why not make this a daily prayer, first thing in the morning: "God, I recognize I have a choice to turn to You or to turn to other things to satisfy my cravings. So I keep asking for Your wisdom to know what to do and Your indwelling power to walk away from things that are not good for me."

Embrace a True Identity

Secondly, the phrase "glorious father" indicates our relationship to God and answers the question, "Why are we made for more?" We are made for more because we are children of God, and this redefines our identity. For years I identified myself by my circumstances. I was "Lysa, the broken girl from a broken home." "Lysa, the girl rejected by her father." "Lysa, the girl sexually abused by a grandfather figure." "Lysa, the girl who walked away from God after the death of her sister." "Lysa, who struggled with looking to friends, boys, and accolades to feel important, special, and loved." "Lysa, who the doctor labeled obese."

Then one day I read a list of who God says I am. I took that list of Scriptures and started to redefine my identity. What a stark contrast to the way I saw myself. I finally realized I didn't have to be defined by my circumstances.

Instead, I could live the reality of who my glorious heavenly Father says I am:

Lysa, the forgiven child of God. (Romans 3:24)

Lysa, the set-free child of God. (Romans 8:1–2)

Lysa, the accepted child of God. (1 Corinthians 1:2)

Lysa, the holy child of God. (1 Corinthians 1:30)

Lysa, the made-new child of God. (2 Corinthians 5:17)

Lysa, the loved child of God. (Ephesians 1:4–5)

Lysa, the close child of God. (Ephesians 2:13)

Lysa, the confident child of God. (Ephesians 3:12)

Lysa, the victorious child of God. (Romans 8:37)

I was made to be set free — holy, new, loved, and confident. If anything sets itself up to negate my true identity, I can't allow myself to partake in it. Whether it's a relationship where someone makes me feel less than my true identity, a college credit card application begging to be filled out so I can purchase things beyond my means, or a vicious food cycle that leaves me defeated and imprisoned, I must remember I was made for more. Remembering this helps empower me to see that living in victory is sweeter than any unhealthy food choice, credit card, or cute guy.

So That You May Know Him Better

Did you catch the reason we need to keep asking for wisdom and revelation, and the real reason for embracing our true identity? It's not just so we can feel better about ourselves. It's not just so we make peace with knowing we're not letting God down. It's not just to help us make healthier choices. It's not even to help us operate as victorious children of

God. (Although these are all wonderful benefits.) There's more. Even though we grow closer to God by redirecting our cravings, we must also see that, in the midst of all the struggle, there's an opportunity for more. For example, you know how you can grow close to a friend through having fun and hanging out, but when you go through a struggle together you get to know them even better. The same is true with God.

The real reason for operating under the truth that we are made for more is, "so that you may know him better." Re-read the Ephesians verses on page 154 and you'll see those seven telling, revealing, beautiful words. The more we operate in the truth of who we are and the reality that we were made for more, the closer to God we'll become.

I don't know about you, but this one benefit alone is worth all the effort, struggle, and sacrifice required along this journey of learning to crave God more. There is a deeper purpose to all this. Making this connection helps this whole adventure become less about what you might give up and more about all you stand to gain with God.

A Hope and Power Like No Other

Isn't this an interesting phrase that comes next — "that the eyes of our heart may be enlightened" to the hope and power that is available to us? Enlightened literally means "to shed light upon."[1] In other words, Paul also asks that light can be shed upon our hearts so that we can more clearly see and use the hope and power available to us.

We would do well to pray for the eyes of our hearts to be enlightened to this hope and power. Throughout this book we've seen that too many times, we try and muster up the gumption to make changes in our lives on our own. So when we do make mistakes it doesn't take long for the dark feelings of discouragement, disillusionment, and defeat to fill our hearts.

In the face of our human frailties, it is crucial for us to have a hope and a power beyond ourselves. In fact, we're built for it: we are made for hope and the same power that raised Christ from the dead. And each time you proclaim, "I am made for more," I pray all the power-packed truths within that statement rush into your heart and keep you enlightened.

We are made for more than excuses and vicious cycles. Even if we have messed up yesterday, we can start to taste success today. We can experience truth. We can choose to stay on the path of perseverance. We can build one success on top of another. We can keep "made for more" on the top of our mind and the tip of our tongue. And we can be totally transformed as we keep asking ... embrace our true identity ... and operate in the hope and power that's like no other.

As I came to understand these verses and many others, I wept with joy and relief, realizing this would be one of the most significant spiritual journeys of my life. A spiritual journey that would yield great benefits as long as I didn't let defeat overtake me.

And what about my concerns with letting God down? My pastor, Steven Furtick, put that to rest one day with a simple but very profound truth: "How can you let God down when you weren't ever holding Him up?"

What a great question! And we find a very clear answer in Isaiah 41:10: "Do not fear, for I am with you; do not be dismayed, for I am your God. I will strengthen you and help you; I will uphold you with my righteous right hand." God is clear that He is the one holding us up, not the other way around.

As we move forward on our journey to conquer our cravings, Part Five of this book will investigate several key principles that will help us greatly on the road. And the first one is to make sure that we direct our thoughts onto the path of truth from the very beginning — because wherever we allow our thoughts to take us, our actions usually follow.

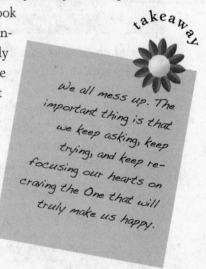

takeaway

We all mess up. The important thing is that we keep asking, keep trying, and keep re-focusing our hearts on craving the One that will truly make us happy.

the action plan

Please take some time this week to memorize a few of these verses to help you define, or in some cases *redefine*, your identity. When your mind starts to think negative thoughts or you begin to feel discouraged, quote these verses as a source of strength, power, and protection. Remembering these truths is one of the most crucial steps toward permanent progress.

(Your name), the forgiven child of God. (Romans 3:24)

(Your name), the set-free child of God. (Romans 8:1–2)

(Your name), the accepted child of God. (1 Corinthians 1:2)

(Your name), the holy child of God. (1 Corinthians 1:30)

(Your name), the made-new child of God. (2 Corinthians 5:17)

(Your name), the loved child of God. (Ephesians 1:4–5)

(Your name), the close child of God. (Ephesians 2:13)

(Your name), the confident child of God. (Ephesians 3:12)

(Your name), the victorious child of God. (Romans 8:37)

I am _____, and I was made for more!

PART FIVE

Principles and Pointers
for the Journey

chapter 16

The Power of New Patterns of Thought

One high school memory haunted me (Lysa) for years. There was a boy I really liked. I mean, I *really* liked him. Like I would write my first name with his last name over and over, daydreaming about the day he'd finally ask me out.

Anyhow, I remember when the lights dimmed at school dances and somewhere between "My Sharona" and "Walk Like an Egyptian" inevitably came the sounds of Hall and Oates, "Your Kiss Is on My List." I had a list and he was at the very top ... You get the picture.

The only problem was that my crush had a list of his own and I not only wasn't at the top, I hadn't even made the cut. To him, we were just friends. Put that little combo together and it was a formula for heartbreak.

Then came the moment that, more than twenty years later, I can still recall as if it happened yesterday. List Boy comes and sits beside me at the school dance. I try to play it cool and act like I'm surprised to see him. Like I hadn't noticed him all night, even though I had secretly kept an eye on his every move since he'd walked in. We exchange chitchat for a few minutes.

We are only speaking very simple words but inside of me a whole different thing is happening. My heart is beating out of my chest; my mind is leaping through pages of our future together — our first dance, our engagement, our wedding. Right as I'm getting around to naming our first three children, he drops a bomb on me.

He says he thinks I'm pretty cute, but it's too bad I have big ankles; otherwise we might be able to go out sometime.

"Excuse me? Did you just say I have big beautiful eyes? I know *ankles* and *eyes* don't sound much alike, but surely you didn't just say *ankles?*"

"No," he replies, "I actually said TANKLES."

Seriously, I could write one of those catchy *High School Musical* singsong-y songs and make millions from this horrid conversation. Picture some sweet, brace-faced girl's head, be-bopping back and forth, her grosgrain ribbons trying to stay on beat with her ponytailed hair. Throw in a zit or two and less-than-model-like legs, and the song would go something like this:

> *He loves me.*
> *He loves me not.*
> *If it weren't for my tankles*
> *he'd think I was hot.*

Seriously ... TANKLES! Why couldn't he have kept this little opinion to himself? I could have just chalked up the fact that he never asked me out to my frizzy hair or my zits or my braces ... All of that would eventually change. But my ankles? Tankles? Well, they would be my constant companion for life.

I eventually matured past my ankles bothering me every minute of every day. Just about the time where they were merely a weekly point of contention, I decided to have a little conversation with God about my ankles. I told Him this was a silly thing to bring up, but I really needed to have a better perspective on the whole tankle-ankle situation.

I think the Lord had actually been eager for me to discuss this with Him. He was quick to answer my question with a question. Not that we had an audible discussion; we didn't. It was just this impression deep in my heart and I know God was speaking to me.

> GOD: "Are you clumsy, Lysa?"
> LYSA: "Yes, Lord. I am very clumsy."
> GOD: "Have you ever twisted your ankle?"
> LYSA: "Never."
> GOD: "Wouldn't it bug you to constantly twist your ankle and be put out of commission?"
> LYSA: "Yes, very much."
> GOD: "Lysa, I have perfectly equipped you with ankles of strength and convenience. Be thankful."

The conversation wasn't as clear-cut and back-and-forth as that, but this is the basic message I received as I sat quietly and prayed about this. Maybe you could try having a similar "quiet time" with God about whatever your tankle equivalent is and see what He reveals to you.

A Biblical Prescription for Fighting the Bad Thoughts

I wish I had let God speak to me about my tankle situation earlier, because that conversation with that boy bred within me a deep insecurity—it shocked me, and seriously messed with my mind and my heart. I imagine that you, too, have things that have messed with your mind and your heart. You may be facing something even now that threatens to derail you; something that has caused you to wonder how you can ever make peace with the realities in your life, your friendships, your background, your family, your body. Perhaps parents, peers, friends, or enemies have purposely or inadvertently hurt you with their comments. And maybe those comments are rattling around in your heart and mind and chipping away at your worth.

After the dance, I allowed the "you would be cute if it weren't for your tankles" theme to rattle around and cause great damage. I internalized it, thinking that "Because this part of me will never change, no boy will ever like me." I was miserable for many years about it, when I didn't have to be.

Girls, there is a biblical prescription that will help you fight those insecure, inferior, formed-in-the-pit-of-a-very-dark-and-fiery-place feelings. I hope you circle this in a bold red pen. That prescription is found in 2 Corinthians 10:5, when the apostle Paul says, "We destroy arguments and every lofty opinion raised against the knowledge of God, and take every thought captive to obey Christ" (ESV).

If there is a feeling, an opinion, a situation that is raised against the knowledge of God's truth and is making us feel insecure, we can't let it go unaddressed. If we do, it risks sinking deeper into our heart. Instead, we have to destroy it. And we do it by "taking every [bad] thought captive" out of obedience to Jesus.

We can literally say to a comment or a thought that presents itself to us, "Are you true? Are you beneficial? Are you necessary?" Okay, it was "true" that I had big ankles, but that wasn't the thought that was killing me. The thought that needed to be destroyed was the next one in line: "No boy will ever like me." That surely could not be true, and it was definitely not beneficial and necessary!

When the answer to those questions is no, we don't hold open the door of our heart and let the thought waltz on in. Instead, we make a conscious choice to "take that thought captive" and destroy it. Imagine yourself living in one of those spaceships in the science fiction movies, and this thought (like "no boy will ever like me") floats in from outer space to bother you. You examine it, realize it is untrue and damaging, and instead of letting it have any access to your mind and heart, you immediately shove it into the airlock. Then you push the button to vent the airlock into outer space and walk away.

That day at the dance, I would have spared myself so much unhappiness if I had taken my dreadful thoughts captive, shut them out, and walked away. I didn't realize it at the time, but I did have a choice: I could (and did) feed that guy's comment and let it grow into an identity crusher, or I could see it for what it was: a careless and insensitive comment by one guy.

One type of choice leads someone to obsess over something negative and become very unhappy. The other leads to shutting out the negative and making room for contentment and peace. I don't know about you, but it is so encouraging to me to realize that we have the *choice* of whether to live with unhappiness or live in peace.

And you have the same choice. You can either feed your sense of unhappiness and discontent by allowing yourself to focus on what your friend said, the size of your clothes, or the size of your (or your parents') bank account. Or, instead, when that sense of inferiority or unhappiness pops up, you can take those thoughts captive and focus instead on the amazing truths of what God says about you.

Replacing the Bad Scripts with the Good Ones

Focusing on God's truths about us is vital, because we can't solely concentrate on shutting out the bad scripts that play in our head about ourselves, or the subtle lies that pop up every time we're tempted. We have to replace the bad and damaging scripts with the good ones, and get into the habit of saying other things.

These are our "go-to scripts," and they aren't just ways to invite God's strength into our weakness. As we repeat these statements, they become new patterns of thought.

You've already seen several of these, but this is a useful summary list. And below each script you'll find an encouraging Scripture verse. You know how we've talked a lot about getting God's truths in us? Well, these verses would be great to add to your list of those to memorize!

1. I was made for more than this unhealthy choice.

   Romans 8:31: "What, then, shall we say in response to this? If God is for us, who can be against us?"

2. When I am considering a compromise, I will think past this moment and ask myself, "How will I feel about this choice tomorrow morning?"

   1 Corinthians 6:19–20: "Do you not know that your body is a temple of the Holy Spirit, who is in you, whom you have received from God? You are not

your own; you were bought at a price. Therefore honor God with your body."

3. When tempted, I will either remove the temptation or remove myself from the situation.

   1 Corinthians 10:13 – 14: " God is faithful; he will not let you be tempted beyond what you can bear. But when you are tempted, he will also provide a way out so that you can stand up under it. Therefore, my dear friends, flee ..."

4. I don't have to worry about letting God down, because I was never holding Him up. God's grace is sufficient.

   2 Corinthians 12:9 – 10: "But he said to me, 'My grace is sufficient for you, for my power is made perfect in weakness.' ... For when I am weak, then I am strong."

5. I have these boundaries in place not for restriction but rather to define healthy parameters for my freedom.

   Romans 6:19: "I put this in human terms because you are weak in your natural selves. Just as you used to offer the parts of your body in slavery to impurity and to ever-increasing wickedness, so now offer them in slavery to righteousness leading to holiness."

The Beauty of Boundaries

Now that we have these scripts and others, how do we use them to create new patterns of thought? Since we've covered the first four already in previous chapters, let's look at script number five: "I have these boundaries in place not for restriction but rather to define the parameters of my freedom."

Does it ever frustrate you when your parents put boundaries on your freedom? I understand. It used to frustrate me when I was a teenager and my parents seemed too strict. But now that I'm a parent, I understand. My parents weren't trying to keep me from a great life. They were trying to keep me *for* a great life.

Just like it might frustrate you that your parents put boundaries around your freedom, maybe that same thing frustrates you about God too. Why can't we eat as much as we want to? Why is it wrong to have sex with your boyfriend if you're in love? Why do we have to give 10 percent of what we earn to God through tithing at church, even when things are tight financially?

Instead of looking at these boundaries from only our perspective, let's look for the bigger picture of why God sets limits for us — and what might be very, very good about them.

I learned this through our sweet little dog, Chelsea. She is not the brightest bulb in the lamp around cars driving down our long driveway. She's obsessed with trying to attack the tires crunching against our gravel drive. As a result, she recently had her second unfortunate encounter with a moving vehicle. In one heart-rending moment, Chelsea was whimpering in intense pain on the driveway, severely banged up with a broken front leg, a terribly scraped-up back leg, and a nose with half the flesh missing.

The vet informed us that in order for her legs to heal properly, we'd have to keep her calm for three weeks. If she was allowed to run around, she might never be able to walk or run properly again. Somehow, we would have to keep her as immobile as possible, locked up in my bathroom the whole time. I asked if he could give her some nerve pills and throw a few in for me too. (I was totally kidding, of course—but, honestly, I thought I could seriously go crazy trying to keep a very active dog calm and immobile. It would be a challenge to keep Chelsea still for three minutes. But three *weeks*?)

Well, two weeks into the healing journey all that stillness got the best of sweet Chelsea in the middle of the night. She decided she would punish me with a fit of whining, crying, and banging against my closed bathroom door. She wanted out and she wanted out *now*. She wanted to run and chase some unsuspecting night creature.

And I wanted her to be able to run and chase a night creature too. Oh, did I ever. It hurt my heart to see her sad, trapped in the bathroom, unable to run and play like she desperately wanted to. It hurt my heart to stick with the doctor's boundaries, gently push her eager little self aside and close the door, and hear her whimpering to get out. But my love for this dog would not permit me to allow her to harm herself. Why did I restrict her freedom? Because I loved her and I could see things she couldn't.

Why do your parents restrict your freedoms? Because they love you and can see things you can't.

And most importantly, why does God restrict your freedoms? Because He loves you and can see things you can't.

Chelsea's brokenness couldn't handle the full freedom she so desperately wanted. So I didn't let her run free.

Not yet.

And as I tossed and turned in the wee hours of that morning, the truth behind that statement about Chelsea's brokenness struck me as quite applicable to myself as well. My brokenness couldn't handle certain kinds of freedom either.

That's precisely why my parents drew clear boundaries when I was young. My biological dad had left our family, which caused brokenness inside me. Without the boundaries set by my mother and stepfather I would have gone looking for a boy's love and affection to replace what was missing. And I would have gotten into all kinds of trouble.

When I went off to college and my parents' boundaries were no longer in place, I *did* get into all kinds of trouble. Why? Because I had never learned how beneficial boundaries are. So I didn't establish them myself.

I'd love to spare you that regret. Go back and read the go-to scripts listed in your journal and this chapter again. Use these to help you respect your parents' boundaries and to start learning to establish boundaries on your own. Trust that there's a bigger picture you can believe in, a better future out there for you.

Eventually, Chelsea's boundaries increased as she healed and learned to properly handle her freedom. The same is true of me. Eventually, I was so thankful God didn't work the miracle I begged Him for with tankles boy. Had He done that I wouldn't be married to the most amazing man named Art, who loves me tankles and all.

takeaway

When I am fighting a hurtful thought that makes me feel bad about myself, I can ask myself: Is this true? Is this beneficial? Is this necessary? If not, I can take that thought captive, shut it out, and walk away. God isn't keeping me from a great life. He's keeping me for a great life.

the action plan

Think of the many boundaries that have been placed in your life, whether they are from your parents, teachers, coaches, bosses, or church leaders. Take the time to write some of these boundaries down.

Now as you look over your list, try to look at these boundaries as safe places. It may be difficult to see your boundaries this way if you've never thought of this concept before. But in time, if we look at our boundaries as gifts from God to keep us safe, our whole perspective on life can change.

Please visit this list one more time — next to each boundary you recorded, write why you are thankful for this boundary.

Have you been able to see a change in your perspective with your boundaries? My prayer is that through this simple exercise you will be able to see your boundaries as parameters that *define* your freedom, not as horrible restrictions *keeping you* from freedom.

chapter 17

Big Things Are Brought Down by Little Things

On January 15th, 2009, US Airways Flight 1549 took off from New York with 155 occupants on board. The takeoff went fine, but three minutes later, at only 3,000 feet, the jet encountered a flock of geese. Both engines were shut down. Captain Chesley Sullenberger—now known by millions simply as "Captain Sully"—had to make a surprisingly successful emergency landing on the Hudson River to save the people onboard.

As I (Lysa) watched this story being covered over and over on the news, I was stunned that mere birds had brought down an Airbus 320. Big things can be brought down by small things.

We would do well to remember this principle in life.

What are some "little'" things that might be posing big dangers in your life right now?

"Not Even a Hint"

Just as Captain Sully didn't see the geese coming toward his engines, often we can be blinded to how some things are a much bigger deal than they appear. We see that principle at work in this verse from Ephesians: "But among you there must not be even a hint of sexual immorality, or of any kind of impurity, or of greed, because these are improper for God's holy people" (5:3).

Hmmm. We can see examples of our three cravings peeking out from this single verse!

Do you see them?

Emotional desires. The desire for affection from boys, taken too far, can lead to sexual immorality.

Physical desires. Junk food, no food, cigarettes, alcohol, and other numbing substances are impurities in our bodies.

Material desires. Spending to oversupply ourselves — especially at the expense of being able to give to God and others — is greed.

What's interesting is the exact phrasing the Bible uses in regard to what amount of immorality, impurity, and greed is acceptable: "Not even a hint!" In other words, not only should we not have these things in our lives, we shouldn't participate in activities that even *hint* in that direction.

Why? Because a hint is starting to flirt with little compromises. Little compromises lead to excuses. Excuses lead to justifications. And justifications lead to trying to get our legitimate needs met in illegitimate ways. Illegitimate ways lead to sinful lifestyle choices. Sinful lifestyles choices always, always, always separate us from God.

And that's exactly where Satan wants us.

Do you see the subtle progression? A hint can quickly turn into a full-blown sinful lifestyle choice that separates us from God. Indeed, big things (the great life God has planned for us) can be brought down by little things (toying with compromises we think are no big deal).

I wish I had read this chapter when I was your age, because some "little" things turned into really big mistakes in my life. And while I eventually got back on track with God and found forgiveness and grace, I suffered the consequences of my choices. I pray that by sharing some of my mistakes in these three "not even a hint" areas, I can help save you from suffering in the same way.

Not Even a Hint of Sexual Immorality

I never had a boyfriend in high school, but in college things changed. I went from never being noticed by boys to suddenly catching the eye of the football team's superstar. The guy every girl wanted to date suddenly wanted to date me. Me! I couldn't believe it.

For the first time in my life I felt beautiful, noticed, and incredibly special.

Never mind that this boy wasn't a Christian. Never mind he partied. Never mind he pressured me to stay over at his place. I brushed aside the warnings and red flags, determined that I would influence him to make better choices.

That didn't happen. Have you ever done the exercise where you stand on a bench and try to pull someone else up to you? It's nearly impossible to pull someone up to where you are. However, if that person attempts to pull you down off the bench, it's much easier.

That's the way it was in our relationship. I didn't pull him up; he only pulled me down. Way down. What started as a thrilling little flirt with slight compromises ended in devastating heartbreak, shame, guilt, and regret.

Not Even a Hint of Impurities

I never drank in high school. Not only was I underage, I'd seen family members drink in excess and I didn't like how it changed them. But when I started dating Popular Football Dude, I started going to the parties he frequented. I started making excuses and justifications that just a little alcohol wouldn't be so bad.

But before I knew it, a little became a lot. The alcohol impaired my ability to make wise choices and think through consequences. It wasn't long before I was living a crazy life-style that wasn't me. It wasn't me at all. I felt distant from God but trapped by my choices. This one impure choice of drinking led to other impure choices in life.

Not Even a Hint of Greed

As my choices changed, I changed. Suddenly, life became all about me. Whatever made me look good and feel good in the moment became my definition of good. On a whim I decided I needed a different car. My parents told me my old car was fine, and with the tuition they were paying they didn't support me getting another car.

I didn't listen.

I went to a used car lot and traded my old, reliable car for a used sports car. I had to work two jobs on top of my already demanding class schedule to keep up with the higher car payments. My grades slipped and my anxiety level skyrocketed, all because of greed.

Greed is an excessive desire to acquire more than you need. I didn't need another car. But this intense desire for something newer, snappier, and more noticeable clouded my ability to think through the consequences of my choice rationally. And when the transmission to my flashy car blew and I had to borrow money from my parents to get it fixed, my greed negatively affected my parents as well.

What If I'm Already Here?

So, back to my question: What are some "little" things posing big dangers in your life right now? Or, what are some little things that have already caused a crash?

Identify them, write them in your journal, confess them to a trusted friend. Because that right there leads to the hope. Unlike Captain Sully, who never saw the geese coming, we can identify the hints of things that lead to compromise.

And if we identify where we're on the slippery slope of compromise, excuses, justifications, and sin, it's never too late to hit the brakes and throw it in reverse. If we identify what little things already brought us down, it's never too late to get back up, repent of the old ways, commit your new way to God, and start to fly again knowing that He sees you as totally clean and pure.

Please hear me — no matter where you are, it's never too late. You've never gone too far that God can't redeem you, restore you, forgive you, and give you a second chance. Though there are ramifications for the choices made, the quicker you turn away from sin, the less severe those consequences will often be.

Never Let Things Fester in Secret

It is important to realize that the slippery slope has one major, telltale sign — things done in secret. The minute we start hiding things from those who love us, doing things in a sneaky way, lying or telling half-truths, and figuring out ways to cover up evidence of our activities, we're on the slope, headed downhill fast.

Satan is the master of darkness. As long as he can keep us operating in our dark secrets, he rules us.

We are reminded in Acts 26:18 to open others' eyes and turn them from darkness to light, and from the power of Satan to God, so that they may receive forgiveness of sins and a place among those who are sanctified by faith in Him. The same holds true for us.

In *The Message*, Acts 26:18 reads:

> I'm sending you off to open the eyes of the outsiders so they can see the difference between dark and light, and choose light, see the difference between Satan and God, and choose God. I'm sending you off to present my offer of sins forgiven, and a place in the family, inviting them into the company of those who begin real living by believing in me.

Oh, sweet friend, we need to see the difference between dark and light and choose light. Bring your choices out into the light of Jesus so He can shine His truth. The choices we most want to hide are the ones we most need to bring into the light and be honest about. That can be hard, but keeping a secret is much, much harder, because you're trapped, stranded in private turmoil. Once it is out in the light, instead of feeling shame you will feel *free*.

There's another very important point to consider: only in the light can we truly discern the difference between being led by Jesus or being led by Satan. And where we do things in secret we are letting ourselves be led, tricked, and undermined by the devil.

Satan keeps dangers off our radar screen and blinds us to the harsh realities coming our way. Just like those geese weren't on Captain Sully's radar screen, but they were there. And when they hit that huge plane, it crashed.

And so will we.

If you're keeping secrets today, bring them out into the light. Get honest with your parents, and ask them to help you hold your choices up to the truth. If there are unusual reasons that make you unable to share with at least one of your parents, find a trusted Christian mentor who is at least ten years older than you. In general, build accountability measures in your life—ask trusted people to ask you about your areas of temptation, and promise that you will be honest in your answers.

Most importantly, ask Jesus for help, forgiveness, and a clear understanding of how to put on the brakes and throw things in reverse. Let His truth speak louder than your feelings begging you to keep things hidden. Like the end of that passage in Acts says, begin real living by believing in Him.

The path to real living—the living that will sustain you and lead you to a true discovery of real love, real provision, and real satisfaction—is found only by following Jesus.

Yes, big things can be brought down by little things. All of us have learned that. But we have also learned that Jesus can resurrect everything brought down by Satan. Consider this wonderful passage from the prophet Isaiah:

> Even youths grow tired and weary,
>   and young men stumble and fall;

but those who hope in the LORD
will renew their strength.
They will soar on wings like eagles;
they will run and not grow weary,
they will walk and not be faint.

Isaiah 40:30–31

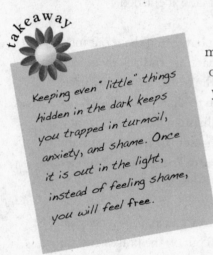

takeaway

Keeping even "little" things hidden in the dark keeps you trapped in turmoil, anxiety, and shame. Once it is out in the light, instead of feeling shame, you will feel free.

Today, we know that you may feel weighed down instead of soaring. You may know that you need to make a change, and really wish you would travel with that kind of freedom. But you may be wrestling with the old desires. You may, secretly, still *want* the pleasure of the illicit relationship, the unhealthy physical habit, or the rush of the newly-filled shopping bags that you hurry to hide in your closet. The next chapter will illuminate a very important principle about all those "wants," that you need to embrace in order to live the truly transparent life the Lord has for you, free of whatever big or little things used to take you down. Remember, the Lord alone is the lifter of your head, the redeemer of your circumstances, and the One who can set you back in flight.

the action plan

Journal your thoughts about this prayer below. Make it your own. Pray it often.

Oh, Lord, unsettle me. Reveal to me where there are areas of my life that mock my desire to be a godly young woman—whether "little" compromises or big ones. Reveal those attitudes that I've wrapped in the lie, "Well, if that's all the bad that's in me, I'm doing pretty good." Help me to allow You to reach the deepest parts of me—dark and dingy and hidden away too long. Teach me to hope that now is the best time to change. Cover me with a deeper love for You and the realization I am made for more than this constant battle.

Lord, unsettle my heart until I'm totally Yours. Amen.

chapter 18

You Crave What You Consume

I (Shaunti) have a confession: I have this little problem involving shopping malls.

If I stay away from the mall, I'm fine. After all, I already have plenty of nice clothes, a house that is overflowing with "stuff," and so many shoes that my husband wonders whether I'll ever be able to see the floor of my closet again. (He has a grand total of three pairs of shoes — one for work, one for casual, and one for running — and looks at me funny when I earnestly explain that I *need* all those shoes for my different speaking outfits.)

So, really, I don't need anything else. Also, since an economic slowdown has taken a big bite out of our budget, and I have to preserve enough money to pay my staff every two weeks, I really *shouldn't* get anything else. And I'm fine with that.

Or I should say, I'm fine with that ... as long as I stick with one of my personal self-discipline "rules" and stay away from the mall altogether.

But the other day I got out of a business meeting early and the next one wasn't for an hour. And there was a mall across the street. *I'll just go sit in the coffee shop over there*, I thought. *I don't want to sit for so long in the lobby of this boring old office building when I can work in a perfectly comfortable coffee shop instead.*

So I drove across—and never even made it to the coffee shop. My own personal lie to myself didn't even get me as far as a token cup of coffee to justify putting myself in a dangerous situation.

Fifty-five minutes later, I was hustling back out to the parking lot with not one, not two, but *four* shopping bags from two department stores, a bookstore, and a kiosk full of sunglasses that reached out and grabbed at my arm while I was walking by. Really.

See, when it comes to the mall, I blow it. I walk into the entrance by the coffee shop, and the hallway kiosk catches my eye, and I think, *Oh, wow, that pair of sunglasses would be great for my speaking trip to Florida next week ... and I need to get a birthday present for Mom, so maybe I should just glance at the department store ... Oh, look at that cute outfit over there—it would be fun to try that on ...*

I didn't want the outfit before I saw it, but as soon as I laid eyes on it suddenly I really wanted it. And when I went further and tried it on, suddenly I really, *really* wanted it.

Changing Your "Want To"

By this point in our journey, you probably have several things you know you need to change, but the problem is that when you are confronted with an actual temptation, you may not be so sure that you *want* to change.

As some wise sage one said, "Opportunity may knock only once, but temptation leans on the doorbell."[1]

So how do you change your "want to"? How do you want to do the right thing and *not* want to do the wrong one? Well, most of us have a fundamental misunderstanding about how our "wants" work. We think we want something, so we go after it. But we need to realize that, usually, it works the other way around. When we go after something, *that* is when our feelings of desire get stronger and we want it far more than we would otherwise.

God designed us in such a way that *our feelings follow our actions*. You will follow what you focus on, and crave what you consume.

For example, you may think that you eat those salty chips because you find them irresistible. But you actually find them irresistible because you have conditioned yourself to be eager for them. You may have never liked Diet Coke much, but then after a month of drinking Diet Coke in your job at the movie theater, suddenly you find yourself craving it each day. If you eat brownies and chips, you'll yearn for brownies and chips in the worst kind of way. You will crave what you eat.

It's that way with everything, not just food. You may think you're intrigued by that bad boy because he has that dark magnetism. But really, you're intrigued because you exchange flirtatious comments with him every day in study hall. You will follow what you focus on.

You may think you want a satchel bag just like your cousin's because it's so cute. But really, you want it because you borrowed it and used it for a whole weekend — and the next time you were at the mall, you walked up to the bag kiosk and took a long look. (Ahem.)

This truth has been apparent since the beginning of

history. After all, Eve craved what she focused on. And as her story shows, our cravings can consume us if we're not careful. Whether we are talking about "consuming" the acceptance of a certain type of friend, something yummy to eat, the feeling of control that comes with *not* eating when you should, or something new that makes you feel improved and puts a bounce in your step, once we taste the forbidden fruit we will crave it worse than we craved it before. We will be *giving* temptation more and more power. And given enough power, temptation will consume our thoughts, redirect our actions, and demand our worship.

This Truth Can Be Powerful — For Good!

Understanding the profound truth that you crave what you consume is not just a warning, of course: it works the same way on the positive side!

When you force yourself to drink water with most meals, instead of cola, you will want water more — in fact, your body may start to crave water on those days you aren't getting enough of it. And when you eat healthy food over a period of time, it seems to reprogram your taste buds. The more veggies and fruit you eat, the more veggies and fruit you crave.

This truth about craving applies to every area of life, not just eating habits. When you *choose* to hang out with Christian friends, instead of the edgy crowd from school, you will want your Christian friends more and the edgy friends less. When you make a habit of tithing 10 percent of your babysitting money to help needy families at your church, you'll feel like something is wrong and missing when you don't — you *want* to give.

Our feelings follow our actions so much, in fact, that our actions become one of the primary tools we have at our disposal as we try to turn our cravings toward God and away from counterfeits. If you really truly want to honor God and change what you are *craving*, you must first change what you are *doing*.

In a way, our cravings—both the healthy ones and the unhealthy ones—are like any living, growing thing. The cravings we feed will grow bigger and stronger, and have more hold on us. But the cravings we starve will wither, weaken, and eventually die. To the degree we "feed" God's way of filling our God-shaped hole, we'll find that way so much more compelling. And to the degree we "starve" all the old, unhealthy ways of filling that hole, we'll find they are much weaker, and have much less power and temptation over us.

But You Must Keep the Momentum Going

Thankfully, once those good choices are a habit, it becomes much easier to keep that momentum going. It is much harder for an isolated mistake or an exception to bump you back onto a bad path. But don't fool yourself. We are sinful people who live in a fallen world, and those unhealthy ways of filling our cravings are only dormant: they aren't dead. I'm sure all of us can recount ways that we have "let our guard down" and have started feeding an old temptation again ... and found it rushing right back in.

Both Lysa and I have seen that our most dangerous time is when we believe we have "conquered" any craving—for example, when we have been so careful with food that we hit our goal weight, or when we have successfully avoided spending and paid off credit card debt, and so on. That time is a blessing entangled with a curse.

The curse is the assumption that freedom now means we can return to some of those things we've given up for so long. We think it's time to celebrate—to live it up!—and invite all those cherished favorites we've missed so much to a little welcome-home party. But we can't welcome home those things without welcoming back everything that comes with them.

This is when the dieter welcomes back all the calories, fat grams, cholesterol, sugars, and addictive additives in her preferred junk food. This is when the meal skipper skips one meal and feels so intoxicated by the hunger it turns into two. This is when the shopaholic goes out for "just one shopping spree" and finds that she's spent $250 on stuff she honestly didn't need. It's when the girl gives into the temptation to go to the movies with the cute rebel guy and his crowd—and afterward finds that he's expecting more in return than she wants to give.

Oddly, when we have our "we've been so strict, we should be able to live it up" party, there is literally a rush of adrenaline and endorphins in our brains. That buzz becomes intoxicating and addictive, and actually makes it harder to be safe the next time. In fact, in the case of food, all the guests we're inviting to our little welcome-home party send out signals to our brain begging us to party with them again and again and again. And then that little welcome-home party becomes a reinvitation to be roommates—which can spell disaster for what we hoped might be a lifestyle change.

Science proves this. For example, several studies have found that certain sugary foods and junk foods actually turn off the body's ability to feel full. Or get this: in a study recently published in *Science News*, researchers found junk food to be measurably addictive in lab rats:

> After just five days on the junk food diet, rats showed "profound reductions" in the sensitivity of their brains' pleasure centers, suggesting that the animals quickly became habituated to the food. As a result, the rats ate more food to get the same amount of pleasure. Just as heroin addicts require more and more of the drug to feel good, rats needed more and more of the junk food. "They lose control," [one of the researchers] says. "This is the hallmark of addiction."[2]

Take it from the lab rats: junk foods are addictive. And so is any unhealthy craving. It's difficult for a girl who has gotten used to certain things in her previous life to uninvite habits, foods, or practices to her party that have been regulars for years. And it's even more difficult to fully grasp that those old habits, foods, or practices aren't our friends.

So do yourself a favor and keep the momentum going. Once you've taken the brave steps of identifying your unhealthy cravings and cutting them out of your life, don't crack the door open for them to creep back in.

God's Exceptions

Although you must choose to keep the momentum going with good choices each day, this isn't about legalism. This isn't following a rule for the rule's sake — it's following the rule because it will help you grow closer to God, honor Him, and satisfy yourself with Him. And that distinction is important, because as you continue on your journey there will almost certainly be exceptions and special occasions when a legalistic rule isn't the answer. In fact, there may be times when rigidly following the right rule might actually be the *wrong* answer.

For example, a while back I realized that I had become undisciplined about my eating during a particularly heavy season of traveling and speaking. I had to be very strict with myself for a few months. And right in the middle of that time of strict cutback, I arrived to speak at a dessert-and-coffee event to find that one of the organizers was a famous master baker, and had created the most astounding cakes for me as the centerpieces of all the desserts at the event. Proudly, the organizers displayed three cakes that looked like they should be on a TV show — and urged me to cut and sample the first pieces.

Now, technically, I should have gently said, "Well, actually, I'm not allowed to have any sugar for the next six days, especially not pieces of three different cakes, but thank you *so* much." But I could tell that this whole group of beaming women were so excited and proud to have me sample the delicious gifts of this famous baker in their midst. That was a case where sticking with the right rule would have been the wrong thing — because it would have truly hurt their feelings. The legalism would have been so unloving. So I did indeed sample pieces of all three of those beautiful cakes.

The things I do for ministry.

And then, of course, I had to be extra vigilant the next few days to get my sugar-stimulated taste buds to settle down and not crave sugar again!

The key, friends, is not to simply follow a rule — it's to be wise about our choices so we rely on God rather than something we crave. There's a very helpful verse we've touched on before in this journey of ours, but it is important to repeat here — this is a verse that you, like us, can seize as a way to sort through the thicket of cravings. Something you can repeat as a very effective go-to script in times of temptation, or as a way to understand the right direction when you're unsure whether to sample a beer at a party, or if you should indulge in the power of spreading a piece of juicy gossip.

> "Everything is permissible for me," — but not everything is beneficial ... I will not be mastered by anything.
>
> 1 Corinthians 6:12

Interestingly, most people associate this verse with sexual sins. However, the very next verse deals with food: " 'Food for the stomach and the stomach for food' — but God will destroy them both" (6:13).

Talk about things that make a girl go *hmmmmm*. The commentary in the *NIV Life Application Study Bible* remarks about these verses, "Some actions are not sinful in themselves, but they are not appropriate because they can control our lives and lead us away from God."[3]

Wisdom Is the Key

The key, friends, is to be wise about your choices. You must stick tight with God, and ask Him to help you understand when a particular choice isn't an "exception" but one that could begin to put you back on a path you know you shouldn't be on. You must be willing to be honest with yourself and recognize when your "but it's a special occasion" excuse is simply one more justification in a string of them. You must be willing to listen to that still small voice of the Holy Spirit that is tapping on your heart about a choice that would tip you into previous patterns of satisfying your cravings outside of God.

Maybe you're asking, "But what does that still small voice sound like?" Great question. It often sounds like Scripture verses we've memorized — God's Word — suddenly popping back into your brain as God's way of reminding you of something you learned. Or it can be a theme or a story from the Bible suddenly coming alive in your life and making you think *Hmmm, this seems familiar. Maybe I should do the same thing that the Bible character did* ... It can also sound like a very simple realization that, "Yes, this is the way." Or it can be that sense that suddenly you feel, "No, no, this isn't right. Not at this time." Deep in your conscience, you will feel one way when something is right and another when it is wrong. Let your conscience receive God's instructions and speak louder than the temptations coming your way.

And, of course, if you feel you can't hear God about a certain issue, ask your mom or dad, or a godly woman in your life who is a bit older and wiser. A godly adult will most certainly be able to help you discern how to stick tight with God.

The good news is that once you do stick tight with God, once you are honest with yourself, once you are willing to listen to that still small voice — you won't want to look anywhere else but to Him.

takeaway

Your feelings will follow your actions. If you want to want the right things, you must first stop doing the wrong ones.

the action plan

In earlier chapters, you listed specific actions you would take to address cravings that were causing a struggle. What have you seen happen in your feelings as a result? In your journal, list the actions, and beside each one describe any ways in which your feelings have changed about that area of struggle.

chapter 19

Beware of "Fair"

In chapter fourteen, I (Lysa) referenced a time when I was on vacation and was tempted to indulge when I knew I shouldn't. Well, let me rewind and tell you the whole story ...

A huge piece of bakery deliciousness was sitting in front of me. It was a combination of three different desserts in one. One layer was cheesecake, one layer was ice cream cake, and in between both of those was a layer of brownie-like chocolate cake ... all drizzled with some kind of fudge icing that was literally calling my name.

This was served to me while my husband, Art, and I were on a special vacation. At the time, I was at the beginning of a no-sugar adventure in my quest to get healthy and shed the weight my doctors said I needed to lose. I'd been doing great at home, but sitting there staring at that dessert was tough. I'd been dropped into a place that was teeming with bakery goodies my mind could not even conceive of, with my husband who could eat a pound of sugar a day and still look fit and trim.

I didn't want Art to miss out so I told him to please enjoy. "I'm fine," I said with a carefree smile. But inside a totally different dialogue was playing in my mind: "It's not fair!"

Maybe you've felt these same feelings. Or maybe your scenario looks different. Perhaps you and your best friends have made plans to go to prom as a group of girlfriends — to simply make it a special girls' night out. Then several of them get asked by boys. They decide they want to go with dates, which leaves you high and dry. You smile and say, "That's okay, I'm fine." But inside, a totally different dialogue is playing out: "It's not fair!"

Or perhaps your best friend asks you to help her pick out a prom dress. You had already decided you were going to use your sister's dress to save money, and were fine with that until your friend starts trying on all these new gowns. Suddenly your borrowed dress doesn't seem so special. You start thinking of all the reasons you don't like your sister's dress, even though you loved it last week. The "it's not fair" dialogue starts screaming in your head as, all the while, you direct fake smiles at your friend.

"It's Not Fair!"

I think the "it's not fair" message is one of the biggest tricks Satan plays to get us to give into temptation. Saying "it's not fair" has caused many a girl to toss aside what she knows is right for the temporary thrill of whatever it is that *does* seem fair. But the next day the sun will rise as it has a habit of doing every day. As each band of light becomes brighter and brighter, the realization of the choice she made the night before becomes clearer and clearer.

Guilt floods her body.

Questions fill her mind.

Self-doubt wrecks her confidence.

And then comes the anger. Anger at herself. Anger at the object of her desire. Anger even at a mighty God who surely could have prevented this.

It's not fair that others can have this, do this, act this way.

> It's not fair I can't buy that new thing I not only want but really feel I need. Just a little debt wouldn't be so bad, right?

> It's not fair I have this body that requires me to eat healthily when that girl eats junk and stays small. Just a couple of pieces of cheesecake wouldn't be so bad, right?

> It's not fair that we can't have sex before we're married when we're so in love. Experimenting can't be so bad when it feels so right, right?

Our flesh buys right into Satan's lie that it's not fair for things to be withheld from us. So we bite into the forbidden fruit and allow Satan to write "shame" across our heart.

Now, I realize that something like a couple of good-night kisses are a small compromise compared to a young girl losing her virginity. But if one night of kissing leads to two nights of groping and that leads to other compromises, which leads to sex, then the downward spiral has led to that loss. Remember how we talked about this earlier? Big things can be brought down by small things.

Also remember: we crave what we consume.

What we focus on the most is what we'll worship. And what we worship will rule us, good or bad.

If we are focused on something other than God, the "poor me" dialogue will fill our mind day after day. Why? Because nothing this world has to offer will ever be enough. Ever. Everything the world tries to get us to replace God with will just leave us more and more dissatisfied. More and more convinced everybody else has it better than us.

Poor me. This isn't fair. I've lived with this struggle for so long. This is a special time. I could just give in this once. Everyone else is doing it.

If we aren't careful to take our thoughts captive, this is when we fall. And then, of course, we are left ashamed and kicking ourselves once more. Which only feeds the poor-me cycle, which feeds the indulgence, which feeds the guilt, which feeds poor-me ...

Stopping the Cycle

In an earlier chapter, we talked about the apostle Paul's famous reminder that God's strength is made perfect in our weakness — and the pity party is surely one of the best examples of a weak time. We think of God's strength as helping us fight temptation, and yes, that is a big application of that particular verse. But *the original reason* that God reminded Paul of this truth was because he was having a pity party about something! Take a look at 2 Corinthians 12:7 – 10 in *The Message*:

> Because of the extravagance of those revelations, and so I wouldn't get a big head, I was given the gift of a handicap to keep me in constant touch with my limitations. Satan's angel did his best to get me down; what he in fact did was push me to my knees. No danger then of walking around high and mighty! At first I didn't think of it as a gift, and begged God to remove it. Three times I did that, and then he told me,
>
> My grace is enough; it's all you need.
> My strength comes into its own in your weakness.

Once I heard that, I was glad to let it happen. I quit focusing on the handicap and began appreciating the gift.

That, right there, is your answer to the pity party: take the thought "it's not fair" captive, and ask yourself "How can this be a gift from God?" How can this be an opportunity to experience God's power firsthand? How can this be an opportunity, over and over, to see God working—and realize that if He worked this time, He'll probably do something pretty amazing next time too? How can this be not a curse, but a *gift*?

Wouldn't it be just like God if we, like Paul, find that He could actually use all these temptations we've been talking about to our advantage? What if having to say no isn't the curse we've thought it to be for so long? What if the thing that tempts us is the very thing that, if brought under control, can lead us to a better understanding of God?

What if we could actually get to the place where, instead of feeling sorry for ourselves, we could *genuinely* thank God for letting us face this battle because of the rich treasures we discovered on the battlefield?

My blog friend E. Titus has struggled with making healthy eating choices and staying at a stable, healthy weight. She sums up what many of us will discover as we stop focusing on the thing we're missing and instead focus on what we're gaining by giving it up:

> When I get all caught up in how unfair it is that my friend is skinny and doesn't have to work at it, how she can eat what she wants when she wants, and how much it stinks that I can't be like her, I remind myself that God didn't make me to be her. You see, He knew even before I was born that I could easily

allow food to be an idol in my life, that I would go to food, instead of to Him, to fulfill my needs. And in His great wisdom, He created my body so that it would experience the consequences of such a choice, so that I would continually be drawn back into His arms. He wants me to come to Him for fulfillment, emotional healing, comfort—and if I could go to food for that and never gain an ounce, well then, what would I need God for?

There is such wisdom in my friend's perspective. Instead of parking her brain in a place where she constantly feels a struggle with the things she craves, she's chosen a much healthier perspective.

No one gets a free pass. Be assured that the person you are envious of, who tempts you to think "it's not fair," is secretly envious of someone else and thinking the same thing.

Realize what that means: the reality of life for the person we compare ourselves to is almost never what it seems. If there's one thing that living forty years has taught Shaunti and me, it's that *everybody* has not-so-great aspects of their lives. Whenever you get an overly idyllic view of someone else's circumstances, remind yourself out loud, "I am not equipped to handle what they have—both good and bad." It's an effective way to stop the pity party in its tracks and help you break the cycle of thinking life isn't fair.

The Good and the Bad

When I want the good things someone has, I must realize that I'm also asking for the bad that comes along with it. It's always a package deal. And usually if I just give a situation enough time to unfold, I thank God I didn't get someone else's package.

One of the first times I came to understand this truth was in middle school when I met a beautiful girl at the children's theater in my town. We were both budding child actors cast in a Christmas play. During rehearsals I remember feeling envious that her long dancer's legs could move in ways my stubby limbs never would. Her legs were muscular and lean and graceful; mine couldn't be described with any of those adjectives.

One day she felt an unusual pain in her left leg. A doctor's appointment turned into a battery of tests that turned into a hospital stay that turned into a diagnosis. Cancer. A surgery to remove a tumor turned into an amputation that turned into a complete life change. Her world became filled with words no child should ever have to know: chemotherapy, prosthetics, hair loss, and walking canes.

As a young girl I was stunned by the whole thing, especially because I clearly remember, night after night, watching her glide across the stage and asking God for legs exactly like hers.

I have learned that I am not equipped to handle what others have — which includes not just the good, but the bad. So the next time we're tempted to start saying, "It's not fair," let's remember the concepts in this chapter. Weaknesses are God's opportunity to reveal His strength working in us. As we say no to things tempting to pull us away from Christ, we'll experience God's power working! Life as a Christ-follower will always be a learning process of depending less on our own strength and more on God's power. The Bible teaches that this "testing of your faith develops perseverance.

Perseverance must finish its work so that you may be mature and complete, not lacking anything" (James 1:3–4).

Oh, this truth should be the cry of our souls instead of Satan's lie that "it's not fair." No one's life is perfect. The more we chase what "they" have, the more empty we'll become. Our cravings for stuff, attention from boys, and unhealthy choices make such empty claims to satisfy us, but only persevering with God will make us truly full, complete, not lacking anything.

And when we get a glimpse of that truth—that astounding, life-changing truth—we will finally be able to take a deep breath and step into the wonderful future and glorious promises that God has for each of us.

takeaway

I am not equipped to handle what she has—which includes not just the good but the bad, and it's always a package deal.

the action plan

List a couple of things you've found (or still find) yourself being envious of in some of your friends, or other people you see. Beside each thing you list, write the takeaway from this chapter, "I am not equipped to handle what she has—which includes not just the good but the bad, and it's always a package deal." Jot a note about what the "bad" might be that God is protecting you from. Pray and ask God to cleanse your heart of jealous feelings. Also, ask the Lord to help you become more and more aware of and thankful for the good in your package deal. The more we focus on being thankful for what we do have instead of sad over what we don't, the more appreciative of God we become.

PART SIX

The Future You Were Made to Have

chapter 20

Being Happy with Me

It is probably a bit silly, but I (Shaunti) love the movie *The Princess Diaries*. There is something in that theme that speaks to every girl and every woman—the idea that we might wake up one day and find out that we have actually been a princess our whole life and didn't know it. And in an earlier chapter, we talked about the fact that we *are* actually daughters of the King—so that does make each of us a princess, if you think about it!

But the main reason I like the movie is something beyond the princess theme: at its core, the story is about something every one of us needs even more. It is the story of a girl, Mia, coming to terms with who she is, and being happy with that.

Initially, she is caught in the trap of *not* being happy with herself, which doesn't change with the newly discovered pedigree. In fact, when Mia finds out that she's a princess, she automatically worries that it'll make her even more of a freak. She gets the professional makeover, and yes, she looks smoother, but she feels just as uncertain inside. She trades riding her scooter to school for being driven in a limo with Joe, the chief of security. But despite all that, one day on the way to school, when her (secretly jealous) best friend stops being kind and starts ragging on her about looking like part of the popular crowd, tears leak down Mia's cheeks. She has the beautiful new hair, makeup, bag, limo, and a castle waiting for her across the ocean, but it doesn't matter—she's not happy with who she is. And her best friend's derision is the final straw.

As they exit the limo, Joe stops her. He has seen the tears leaking down her cheeks. He says something like, "Did my eyes deceive me or did I see tearing back there?"

She tries to tell him she's fine, and he answers, "Very well ... But just remember, no one can make you feel inferior without your consent."

She nods slowly. "Eleanor Roosevelt said that."

"Yes, another special lady like yourself."

It is a turning point for her—and it can be a turning point for any of us.

No one and nothing can make you feel inferior without your consent.

This applies to anything we care about, any area in which we deeply want peace in our emotional, physical, or material cravings, but are finding pain arise instead. No derision from a friend, no number on the scale, no rejection from a guy, no trouble with making the grade in class, no inability to afford the gadgets your friends have—none of that can make you feel inferior without you allowing it to do so.

Why You Are Made the Way You Are

That, of course, may sometimes seem easier said than done. It's hard to remember it when you feel like you just want to crawl away and die. Remember the "tankles" story that Lysa told earlier?

Yeah. We've been there.

But then again . . . remember what Lysa felt God told her about *why* He made her with nice sturdy ankles? It may be hard to pull yourself out of a spiral, but even in the hardest situation you can ask God to help you gain contentment by not just "putting up with" certain things about yourself, but by asking for His help to notice and embrace the reasons why God made you just the way you are.

After all, remember the wonderful promise God gives us in Ephesians 2:10: "For we are God's workmanship, created in Christ Jesus to do good works, which God prepared in advance for us to do."

Let's really *think* about what that means. God looked down through history and knew exactly what He was going to call you to do with your life once you were born — and He created you in such a way that you would be the perfect person to fulfill those callings.

For example, just imagine the Master Creator saying to Himself, *"Well, when this girl is thirty years old, she is going to be called upon to tackle a big business deal that will subtly change the course of an important company I have plans for, so let Me give her a head for math, and add a dash of persever-ance into her personality. But she also will have a husband with a very tender heart, so that means I will need to teach her trust and patience, lest she shred him (and her marriage) without realizing it. Oh, and when her kids get older I am going to bring her an exciting opportunity to travel and train others in her business, and in doing so meet many people who will be drawn to Me through her, so I also need to work into her a teaching gift and a sweet spirit — a spirit that she will develop as she learns to look at the positive instead of dwelling on her disappointment with not being naturally athletic like her sister . . ."*

There is no way that we, with our human minds, can ever know what this glorious, divine process really looks like, but look at the Ephesians 2:10 verse again. God has designed you just the way you are to be able to do specific things that He created in advance for *you* to do. You.

We've heard "God designed you just the way you are for a reason" so often it bounces off our brains. But stop the thought from bouncing, and instead grab it tight and let it sink in.

Begin to imagine—just imagine—that there might possibly be a wonderful, amazing reason why you are made the way you are.

No matter what, you can be assured that there is no true or accurate reason to feel inferior, unwanted, not special, or unhappy with who you are.

Now, make no mistake: we are never going to be perfect people, and every one of us has things we do indeed need to work on. After all, a sense of being unsettled or convicted is God's way of tugging at our hearts and directing us onto His true path for our lives. For example, if I am unhealthy, it is completely legitimate and important to feel unsettled with that, and to want to be healthy instead. If I realize, deep down, that I'm gossiping and criticizing instead of being someone people like to hang out with, it is legitimate and important to want to learn how to be a better friend. But there will never be a legitimate reason to feel worthless or like a mistake.

Our New Measuring Stick

The problem is, in this world it is so easy to look at all worldly things for signals of how we should feel about ourselves. We look to all the measuring sticks of this world for whether we should feel happy with ourselves or feel inferior, lacking, unhappy. (Are my friends including me? When I have a secret crush, does he seem to notice me or ignore my existence? Do I fit into the clothes I want ...?) But the Bible says that all those things will fade as quickly as the morning mist disappears when the sun comes up.

And while looking at the purposeful way God made us, and learning to be content with that, is an excellent thing — even that isn't God's primary measuring stick.

God uses a very different measuring stick for determining whether we should be happy with ourselves — and we need to adopt this measuring stick as our own.

God says *we should be happy with ourselves as we learn to look and act more and more like Him*. The Bible calls this "living a godly life" and "sharing his divine nature," and says that *this* is what should thrill us. It's not just accepting that God made us for a purpose, but obediently living out that purpose.

Best of all, God promises that becoming more like Him is possible! Here's how the apostle Peter presents this truth:

> His divine power has given us everything we need for life and godliness through our knowledge of him who called us by his own glory and goodness. Through these he has given us his very great and precious promises, so that through them you may participate in the divine nature and escape the corruption in the world caused by evil desires.
>
> For this very reason, make every effort to add to your faith goodness; and to goodness, knowledge; and to knowledge, self-control; and to self-control,

perseverance; and to perseverance, godliness; and to godliness, brotherly kindness; and to brotherly kindness, love. For if you possess these qualities in increasing measure, they will keep you from being ineffective and unproductive in your knowledge of our Lord Jesus Christ ... For if you do these things, you will never fall.

2 Peter 1:3–8, 10

That's a lot of text, so let me summarize the principles in these verses that relate to our struggles with our cravings, and our happiness with ourselves:

- God Himself has given us everything we need to triumph over our cravings.
- Above all, we are to reflect a divine nature — to have a secure identity in Christ, and be happy with that. *That* is what will help us escape the corruption of the world and avoid evil desires.
- Having a healthy attitude toward friends, guys, food, body image, or material things is not just about having faith, goodness, and knowledge. We have to add to that foundation by choosing to be self-controlled and choosing to persevere. We need to stay focused on loving others (rather than being self-focused) even when the journey gets really hard.

If we make the choice to be Jesus girls who offer our willingness to exercise self-control and perseverance to the glory of God, we can become healthy in our choices and our friendships. We can escape the cycle of failing and doing it wrong again. We can be victorious and happy with who God made us to be. If we're disappointed with ourselves in some way, especially if there really is something we need to work on, we can look at it and accept it as an indication of our current situation, and not as an indication of our worth.

Think about that last statement. No one and nothing can make you feel inferior or unhappy with yourself without your consent. You can look at something and *accept it as an indication of your current situation and not as an indication of your worth.*

That means we can step on the scale and see the numbers as an indication of how much our body weighs, not as an indication of our worth.

We can hear a friend say something mean about us and see it as an indication of a friend making a rotten choice, and not as an indication of our worth.

We can realize that we just blew our entire summer vacation budget in one ill-advised shopping spree and see it as an indication of an area of sin that we still need to address, not as an indication of our worth.

So if we aren't supposed to define how we feel about ourselves and how we are doing by any worldly standard, and instead by whether or not we look more and more like Jesus … how do we do that? What measuring stick *do* we use?

Happiness from Obedience

What sums up our new measuring stick is captured by a blog post that I (Lysa) saw from my friend Karen Ehman. For years, Karen's main struggle wasn't with the approval of others, or a craving to feel new and improved by sporting the latest clothes or jewelry; it was with not taking care of herself, physically, out of depression or inertia. Now, although her story involves just one type of physical craving, it can be applied to *any* issue that we face.

You see, a few years before, Karen had woken up to her need in this area, and had worked hard to get healthy — she got more fit, and lost over 100 pounds.

But then there came an extraordinarily difficult time of her life, and the pounds began creeping back. She knew it was time to get serious again, but boy was it hard the second time around. She knew some things would have to be different this time, the biggest being that she had to shift her motivation from the delight of seeing the diminishing numbers on the scale to the delight of obeying God.

Her breakthrough — and our lesson — came when she was faced with one of those disappointing situations: after a week of being very careful and self-disciplined, she stepped on the scale, excited to see how much weight she had lost — and discovered it was a tiny amount. She was tempted to be depressed about herself, throw in the towel, and go back to pigging out on whatever was in the pantry to (temporarily) soothe her hurting heart. But then she felt like God pulled her up short and told her something profound:

Define your week by obedience, not by a number on the scale. Here is what she said in her blog:

> The scale does help measure our progress, but it can't tell us everything … So, I had to stop and ask myself the following questions:
>
> - Did I overeat this week on any day? No.
> - Did I move more and exercise regularly? Yes.
> - Do I feel lighter than I did at this time last Wednesday? Yes.

- Did I eat in secret or out of anger or frustration? No.
- Did I feel that, at any time, I ran to food instead of to God? Nope.

Before I hopped on the scale, did I think I'd had a successful, God-pleasing week? Yep!

So, why oh why do I get so tied up in a stupid number? And why did I almost let it trip me up and send me to the kitchen for a 750-calorie binge?

Sweet friends, we need to define ourselves by our obedience, not a number on the scale.

Okay?

Pinky promise?

Good.

We are all in this thing together.

That is so important, girls, and there are so many ways this can apply:

I am defined by my obedience, and not by a number on the scale — or what size my clothes are or how I feel when certain models from a certain company prance across my TV proclaiming Victoria has a secret. I am eating healthy and exercising, and it's okay that I will never look like Victoria or any of her friends.

I am defined by obedience, and not by whether or not I currently have a boyfriend to put his arm around me in the hall at school, or text back and forth with when I'm lonely. I'm doing well at keeping my boundaries with the guys I have gone out with, and creating good friendships, and I'm proud of myself for that.

I am defined by obedience, and not by the fact that my friends went to a movie without me. I have been a good friend to them, but I have refused to give into their desire to gossip about everyone else. If that means some people think of me as "less cool," they probably aren't real friends anyway, and I will continue to concentrate on those who are.

I love the truth that we are to be defined by obedience in every area of our cravings—emotional, physical, and material. Remember, God says *we should be happy with ourselves as we learn to look and act more and more like Him.*

Anything else we could get satisfaction from, or define ourselves by, is temporary; if we hitch our souls to the pursuit of those fleeting things, we'll quickly become disillusioned and more and more unhappy. The only true satisfaction we can seek is the satisfaction of being obedient to the Lord and resting in our identity as Jesus girls.

takeaway

I am a Jesus girl who is defined by obedience, not by a hurtful comment or a disappointing outcome. Those are merely an indication of someone's opinion or my current situation, and not an indication of my worth.

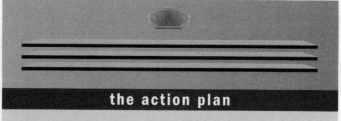

the action plan

In your journal, write a list of all the good things about yourself—all of the positive attributes God has given you, and that you are living up to. In particular, consider those attributes, choices, and ways of living that are consistent with this thought: "I am a daughter of the King, and what will make me happy with myself is when I look and act more and more like Him."

chapter 21

What We Wish

If you could look ten years down the road into your future, what do you hope you'd see? Where would you want to be living? Who would you want to be going through life with? What would you hope your job would look like? And if you had all of this in ten years, what feeling would it give you?

As a young woman I (Lysa) always thought the secret of happiness was growing up, getting a good education for a steady job, finding Mr. Right, building a nice house with flower pots out front, and having kids.

I arranged everything in my life around those goals. Goals are important, and they sure did keep me motivated. But the path I took to get to my goals led me down some pretty treacherous routes. Eventually I had everything I ever thought would make me happy, and I was more miserable and empty than I'd ever been.

Why?

Because I followed my wants, desires, and cravings instead of God.

My most important thing in life was chasing what I thought would make me happy. If it *felt* right, I reasoned it *was* right. But that's such a dangerous way to live. Our feelings should be indicators, not dictators. In other words, our feelings (our heart) can help us gauge what we're experiencing and what is valid in that sense. But our feelings should never dictate our decisions. We're shown this contrast in the Bible in Jeremiah 17. Verse 8 describes the person who relies on truth to lead the way:

> He will be like a tree planted by the water
> that sends out its roots by the stream.
> It does not fear when heat comes;
> its leaves are always green.
> It has no worries in a year of drought
> and never fails to bear fruit.

Verse 9 warns people who are tempted to rely on their feelings to lead the way:

> The heart is deceitful above all things
> and beyond cure.
> Who can understand it?

During all those years I was chasing after what felt right, and had not yet learned how important it was to follow truth, I set God aside. Oh, I called myself a Christian and satisfied that label by going to church when it was convenient and praying before meals. But I wasn't a Christ-follower. I was a self-follower, and there's a big difference between the two.

In our main focus group with young women for this book, the question I most desperately wanted to ask was this: "Do you really believe it's possible to be satisfied by your relationship with God?" After all, this book is titled, *Made to Crave: Satisfying Life's Deepest Desires with God.* So, is that possible?

You may remember I mentioned this in an earlier chapter, but I want to revisit this now that we're nearing the end of our time together. The girls agreed it is possible, but were quick to add, "However, we don't know how."

You see, throughout these pages we've given you a great recipe for craving God and finding satisfaction in Him. A recipe of Truth—God's truth. But as we leave you, you'll have to take this recipe and use it to make a life.

You have a crucial choice to make. Will you follow the recipe of Truth, making decisions based on God's Word? Or will you follow the recipe of temptation, making decisions based on how you feel?

Truth leads you to God's best.

Temptation leads you away from God's best.

Truth leads to satisfaction.

Temptation leads to insatiable hunger.

Truth leads into a deeper walk with God.

Temptation leads to becoming more distant from God.

Recipe for Disaster

So there I was with everything I thought would make me satisfied ... and feeling more hungry than I'd ever been. I was trying to get filled up with things and people. I was walking around with a little heart-shaped cup, holding it out to other people and things, trying to find fulfillment. I held out my cup to food and tried to quiet the cravings of my soul with chips and chocolate that couldn't go any further than my bloated stomach. I held my cup up to my husband and tried to demand he love me in ways that would right my wrongs and fill up my insecurities. I held my cup up to stuff and overspent trying to decorate my home and clothe my body in ways that made me feel pretty.

But nothing worked.

Eventually, I had to admit that. I had followed temptation's recipe — always bouncing from what felt good in the moment but left me empty just a short time later.

Something had to change. It was me.

I love this verse from the Old Testament where God tells the wandering Israelites to go in a different direction: "You have circled this mountain long enough. Now turn north" (Deuteronomy 2:3, NASB).

Whatever our situation, if we are really going to stop circling the mountain and head north toward lasting changes, we have to empty ourselves of the lie that other people or things can ever fill our hearts to the full. Even now, years later, when I'm following the recipe for Truth, I have to keep checking myself to make sure I'm not being lured away.

We have to deliberately and intentionally fill up on God's truths and stand secure in His love. The more I fill myself up with the truths of God's love, the less I find myself pulling out that little heart-shaped cup. I have to mentally replace the lies using some of my favorite verses to remind myself of just how filling God's love really is.

You can do that too! Here are some examples of how each type of craving could play out. Recognize the lie, take that thought captive, and replace it with truth — the biblical truth that we can also soak in through God's Word:

Emotional

Old Lie: I need to text that boy before I go to sleep. I know I shouldn't be talking to him right now, but

I like his confidence and the things he says. Maybe he'll still be up, and maybe what he texts me back will make me feel special and more secure.

New Truth: The thought that a boy's words will fill me is a lie. He might make me feel good for just a few minutes; I don't need to be puffing up my heart with the empty compliments and conversations of a boy who may or may not stay a part of my life or who doesn't match my spiritual convictions. If I truly need reassurance right now, I am capable of reading my Bible, praying to God, or reading a book that reminds me of God's truths.

Verse to Remember: "And I pray that you, being rooted and established in love, may have power, together with all the saints, to grasp how wide and long and high and deep is the love of Christ, and to know this love that surpasses knowledge—that you may be filled to the measure of all the fullness of God" (Ephesians 3:17–19).

Material

Old Lie: I am such a failure. I spend more than I make and don't know how to stop. The rush of getting new things and having that instant gratification is just too powerful for me. Even if I stop for a while, I know eventually I'll just go back to my old habits anyhow.

New Truth: I am not a failure. I am a lavishly loved child of God. Part of my right as a child of God is to operate in a power beyond myself. The Holy Spirit, God's gift to me, makes it possible for me to use the self-control I've been given.

Favorite Verse: "How great is the love the Father has lavished on us, that we should be called children of God! And that is what we are!" (1 John 3:1).

Physical

Old Lie: God seems so far away, and french fries are right around the corner at the drive-thru.

New Truth: French fries don't love me. And the only lasting thing I get from them is the cholesterol and fat they inevitably leave behind, which will just pollute my body. God's love is here in this moment and in many more moments to come. His love is true and carries with it only positive residual effects.

Favorite Verse: "But from everlasting to everlasting the LORD's love is with those who fear him" (Psalm 103:17).

Old Lie: I am not thin enough. I need to stop eating.

New Truth: My worth is not based on my appearance or weight. God made me, and He doesn't make mistakes! In order to be healthy, I need nourishment.

Favorite Verse: "All beautiful you are, my darling; there is no flaw in you" (Song of Solomon 4:7).

This is just a start toward replacing the lies and rationalizations with the truths of God's love. I encourage you to write out some old lies and new truths on your own. The process of stripping away old lies is hard and can produce raw feelings. That's why it's so crucial to have truths with which to replace them.

When I posted a small portion of these thoughts on my

blog, I received some very vulnerable and honest responses. But one especially grabbed my heart, because Kim is seeing how beneficial replacing old lies with truths can be. She said:

> What you wrote today was clearly from God for me to hear. Since I was twelve years old, I've been trying to get someone to fill me, love me, need me, make me worthy, all in an effort to compensate for the abuse — mental, emotional, and physical — and then complete abandonment of my father, brother, and paternal side of the family.
>
> Food? Honey, let me tell you that 350 pounds later, I am finally getting that food is not a substitute for God's love. It's almost destroyed me. Here I am twenty-eight years later, and my marriage is in shambles; we separated this past Friday. Our five-year-old daughter is stressed, acting out; you name it, she is there.
>
> This is not the life I want. This is not the life I plan to continue to lead. If ever God spoke to me, what you wrote today went right to the heart of the matter. Thank you for being faithful. Thank You, God Almighty, for loving me. I am one step into a future that has real hope — hope that God fulfills.

I pray we are all with Kim on this journey of replacing lies, embracing truth, and learning that other things were never meant to fulfill the deepest places of our hearts reserved for God alone. God says, "See, I have placed before you an open door that no one can shut" (Revelation 3:8). May it be that we walk through that door, head north, and never look back.

Fulfillment in Relationship with God

For me, this starts with taking off my mask before the Lord and asking Him to help me find fulfillment in my relationship with Him.

That's right. Just like all the teenage girls in our main focus group, I had to admit to God, "I want to find satisfaction in the deepest parts of my heart with You and You alone, Lord. But I don't know how. Will You show me how?"

Eventually, I found exactly what I needed — prayers where I don't speak at all.

I had reduced my prayer life to simply praying about my problems. God was who I turned to when nothing else worked. Sad, but true. I'd slipped into a habit of offering up circumstance-oriented prayers where I'd list every problem and ask God to please fix them. I even made suggestions for solutions in case my input could be useful. But nothing changed.

In a huff one day, I sat down to pray and had absolutely no words. None. I sat there staring blankly. I had no suggestions. I had no solutions. I had nothing but quiet tears and some chocolate smeared across my upper lip. Eventually, God broke through my worn-out heart. A thought rushed through my mind and caught me off guard: *I know you want Me to change your circumstances, Lysa. But, right now I want to focus on changing you. Even perfect circumstances won't satisfy you like letting Me change the way you think.*

I didn't necessarily like what I heard during this first time of silently sitting with the Lord, but at least I felt I was connecting with God. And so, to keep that connection, I started making it a habit to sit quietly and listen.

Sometimes I cried. Sometimes I sat with a bad attitude. Sometimes I sat with a heart so heavy I wasn't sure I'd be able to carry on much longer. But as I sat, I pictured God sitting there with me. He was there already and I eventually sensed that. I experienced what the apostle Paul taught when he wrote, "In the same way, the Spirit helps us in our weakness. We do not know what we ought to pray for, but the Spirit himself intercedes for us with groans that words cannot express" (Romans 8:26).

As I sat in silence, the Spirit interceded with perfect prayers on my behalf. I didn't have to figure out *what* to pray or *how* to pray about this situation that seemed so consuming; I just had to be still and sit with the Lord. During those sitting times I started to discern changes I needed to make — God quietly dropped them into my heart. I knew they were from God when these three things were true about what I was sensing Him saying:

1. They lined up with Scripture. Either I needed to find a Bible verse that verified the truth of what I was hearing, or I asked a trusted friend or mentor who knew a lot about the Bible to verify this thought was biblical.

2. It was convicting but not condemning. God does convict us to make changes. These convictions are about issues in my life and lead to positive changes. God doesn't condemn. Condemning statements attack me personally instead of the issues; They shut me down and make me feel worthless. Convictions compel me to change.

3. This would please God. Whenever I ask the question,

"Would this please God?" it weeds out potentially dangerous thoughts I would come up with myself.

On the last one, we would suggest that if you're not sure whether or not God would be pleased with something, get people more mature in their faith involved, like your mom or your youth leader. In other words, you might think you should stop eating for a season to control your weight. But when you ask your youth leader if this would please God, they remind you God wants us to treat our bodies like a temple, which means caring for it and providing what it needs to stay working properly. God would never ask you to starve yourself. Ever. On the other hand, God might ask you to stop turning to junk food in an effort to numb a longing in your heart and instead turn to Him through prayer and journal writing. And when you do, you hear Him guiding you how to redirect your wants and temptations to please Him.

Thankfully—amazingly—when we are submitted to and listening to God regularly, He can and often does use our "wants"—I found that when I was living a submitted life, and in those quiet times with Him He would put His desired direction in my heart and it would become my own.

In that process, I also started to understand how Jesus could be the one to satisfy my deepest longings. I discovered it, and so can you.

So, that's where our journey will end. With you, sitting with Jesus. It's been such an honor for Shaunti and me to hold your hand through this part of your journey. We now take your hand and safely place it within the nail-scarred clasp of His.

This is what we want you to remember:

You are young with eyes that spark and speak of innocence. Don't trade. Don't trade the pure peace that greets you each morning for a taste of something this world tries to offer.

Be wise with possessions. Wait. Wait for generosity's freedom. Always despise greed's lure. Never let that which you possess begin to possess you.

Be wise with physical pleasures. Pause. Pause to consider if this is truly beneficial even when it's permissible. Never let that which you consume, consume you.

Be wise with emotional desires, especially with the boy you let into the inner places of your heart. Be patient. Patient for later. Later, when a guy comes along that will want nothing more than to protect you. He won't want *from* you. He will want *for* you.

For you.

This is what we wish for you:

No matter where you are, let grace wash away the mistakes of yesterday. Journey from here with Jesus. Always, always, with Jesus. Your peace. Your perfect way. The only satisfaction for the deep places within. The One whom you were made to crave.

He will show you. Yes, wait. Pause. Be patient.

This is what we wish.

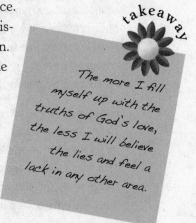

takeaway

The more I fill myself up with the truths of God's love, the less I will believe the lies and feel a lack in any other area.

the action plan

Read the prayer below and tweak it to make it your own. Write it out and read it aloud often. Let it be your heart cry and your soul's joy.

Dear Jesus,

I have finally found the courage to admit I've craved other things and other people more than You. I have wept over losing friends and boyfriends while hardly giving a thought to You losing Your life for me. I've been restless, dissatisfied, and convicted to change but not willing to put forth the effort to do so. I've made excuses. I've pointed fingers. I've been frustrated by my parents trying to put boundaries in my life.

I've relied on material possessions, emotional relationships, and physical comforts for things none of these could ever give me. I've lied to myself about what's really important. I've settled and excused and made pithy comments justifying my issues. I've been enthralled by Facebook while yawning through Your Holy Book.

For all that, I am so sorry. These are not just little issues. These, for me, are sins — missing the mark of Your best for my life. With my whole heart, mind, and soul, I repent. I stand on this step and stare at my reality and turn. I turn from my self-following mindset. I turn from what I must give up and weep no more. I remove my toe from keeping open the door to my old habits and patterns, my old mindset, my old go-to scripts.

I choose freedom. I choose victory. I choose courage. And yes, above all else, I choose You.

And then I'll choose You again.

For now I know: I was made to crave. I was made to get my deepest desires met by You and You alone.

Amen. And Amen.

Acknowledgements

This book has been both an intensely personal project for each of us, as well as one that has come during a very busy season of ministry in each of our lives. We would surely have gone stark raving mad if it weren't for the help and support of a lot of groups of people, including our publisher, prayer teams, amazing staff members, and especially our wonderful husbands and children. We want to specifically acknowledge and thank Jenny Reynolds for so willingly sharing her wise counseling expertise, especially in the area of eating disorders, and Holly Good and Meredith Brock for jumping in with the structure and editing needed from beginning to end. Our thanks also go out to the many teenage girls who helped us by participating in our focus groups, sharing their insights, and commenting on early versions of the manuscript—especially Hope TerKeurst, Sisi Heidorn, and Kaleigh Newby. As always, we have serious heroines on our staff teams who have kept all the plates spinning when we needed to focus on this book, especially our staff directors: LeAnn Rice on Lysa's team and Linda Crews on Shaunti's. At Zondervan, we thank Jacque Alberta for her editing skill and her patience with trying to coordinate the schedules of two busy authors in order to somehow, actually, get a book finished so it can get out the door and onto shelves!

Most importantly, we are so grateful that this project has challenged us anew to stick close to the One who wants to speak directly to you, the reader. In our imperfect way, we hope we have allowed you to hear the voice of your Heavenly Father calling to you in these pages. May all of us, always, crave Him and Him alone.

Notes

Chapter 2: What's Your *That?*
1. From the article "Talking about Idolatry in the Post-Modern Age" (The Gospel Coalition, April 2007). As cited on *www.monergism.com/postmodernidols.html*

Chapter 4: The Emotional Craving
1. Taken from *For Young Men Only: A Guy's Guide to the Alien Gender,* by Jeff Feldhahn, Eric Rice, and Shaunti Feldhahn (Sisters, Oregon: Multnomah Books, 2008), 50.
2. Ibid., 53

Chapter 5: The Physical Craving
1. *The Chronicles of Narnia: The Voyage of the Dawn Treader.* Twentieth Century Fox, 2010.

Chapter 7: Four Reality Checks
1. Taken from *For Young Women Only,* by Shaunti Feldhahn and Lisa A. Rice (Multnomah Books, 2006), 121.

Chapter 9: Tattooed On My Heart
1. Matthew 4:10.

Chapter 15: What If I Let God Down?
1. Definition taken from *www.dictionary.reference.com/browse/enlightened*

Chapter 18: You Crave What You Consume
1. Author unknown.
2. Quote taken from *www.sciencenews.org/view/generic/id/48605/title/Junk_food_turns rats_into_addicts*
3. *Life Application Study Bible (NIV)* footnote for 1 Corinthians 6:12 (Grand Rapids: Zondervan, 2004), 2070.

About Lysa TerKeurst

Lysa TerKeurst is a wife to Art and mom to five priority blessings named Jackson, Mark, Hope, Ashley, and Brooke. The author of more than a dozen books, including the *New York Times*-best selling *Made to Crave*, she has been featured on *Focus on the Family*, *Good Morning America*, the *Oprah Winfrey Show*, and in *O Magazine*. Her greatest passion is inspiring women to say yes to God and take part in the awesome adventure He has designed every soul to live. While she is the cofounder of Proverbs 31 Ministries, to those who know her best she is simply a car-pooling mom who loves her family, loves Jesus passionately, and struggles like the rest of us with laundry, junk drawers, and cellulite.

WEBSITE: If you enjoyed this book by Lysa, you'll love all the additional resources found at *www.MadetoCrave.org*.

BLOG: Dialog with Lysa through her daily blog, see pictures of her family, and follow her speaking schedule. She'd love to meet you at an event in your area! *www.LysaTerKeurst.com*.

A Gift Just for You

Get this free colorful magnet to keep you inspired and on track. The only charge is $1.00 for shipping and handling. Order by emailing: *Resources@Proverbs31.org* and put "Made to Crave Magnet" in the subject line. Bulk orders for Bible studies and small groups are also available with special shipping rates.

To download other free inspirational sayings, be sure to visit *www.MadetoCrave.org*, where you'll find many additional resources.

About Proverbs 31 Ministries

If you were inspired by *Made to Crave* and yearn to deepen your own personal relationship with Jesus Christ, I encourage you to connect with Proverbs 31 Ministries. Proverbs 31 Ministries exists to be a trusted friend who will take you by the hand and walk by your side, leading you one step closer to the heart of God through:

- *Encouragement for Today*, free online daily devotions
- The *P31 Woman* monthly magazine
- Daily radio program

To learn more about Proverbs 31 Ministries, contact Holly Good (*Holly@Proverbs31.org*), or visit *www.Proverbs31.org*.

Proverbs 31 Ministries
616-G Matthews-Mint Hill Road
Matthews, NC 28105
www.Proverbs31.org

Becoming More Than a Good Bible Study Girl

Lysa TerKeurst
President of Proverbs 31 Ministries

Is Something Missing in Your Life?

Lysa TerKeurst knows what it's like to consider God just another thing on her to-do list. For years she went through the motions of a Christian life: Go to church. Pray. Be nice.

Longing for a deeper connection between what she knew in her head and her everyday reality, she wanted to personally experience God's presence.

Drawing from her own remarkable story of step-by-step faith, Lysa invites you to uncover the spiritually exciting life we all yearn for. With her trademark wit and spiritual wisdom, Lysa will help you:

- Learn how to make a Bible passage come alive in your own devotion time.
- Replace doubt, regret, and envy with truth, confidence, and praise.
- Stop the unhealthy cycles of striving and truly learn to love who you are and what you've been given.
- Discover how to have inner peace and security in any situation.
- Sense God responding to your prayers.

The adventure God has in store for your life just might blow you away.

Available in stores and online!

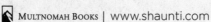

Talk It Up!

Want free books?
First looks at the best new fiction?
Awesome exclusive merchandise?

We want to hear from you!

Give us your opinions on titles, covers, and stories.
Join the Z Street Team.

Email us at zstreetteam@zondervan.com
to sign up today!

Also—Friend us on Facebook!

www.facebook.com/goodteenreads

- Video Trailers
- Connect with your favorite authors
- Sneak peeks at new releases
- Giveaways
- Fun discussions
- And much more!